HEADS

HEADS

Business
Lessons
from an
Executive
Search
Pioneer

RUSSELL S. REYNOLDS, JR.
WITH CAROL E. CURTIS

NEW YORK   CHICAGO   SAN FRANCISCO
LISBON   LONDON   MADRID   MEXICO CITY   MILAN
NEW DELHI   SAN JUAN   SEOUL   SINGAPORE
SYDNEY   TORONTO

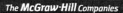

1 2 3 4 5 6 7 8 9 10   DOC/DOC   1 8 7 6 5 4 3 2

ISBN   978-0-07-179500-5
MHID   0-07-179500-6

e-ISBN   978-0-07-179501-2
e-MHID   0-07-179501-4

McGraw-Hill books are available at special quantity discounts to use as premiums and sales promotions or for use in corporate training programs. To contact a representative, please e-mail us at bulksales@mcgraw-hill.com.

This book is printed on acid-free paper.

To Debbie

CONTENTS

CONTENTS

CHAPTER 7

The Birth of RSR Partners   115

CHAPTER 8

Executive Search Today   131

CHAPTER 9

Mastering Being Recruited   155

CHAPTER 10

Equilibrium   183

Index   203

i-xii-001-202_Reynolds.indd   8   5/3/12   4:50 PM

PREFACE

I've tried to write a book about my unbelievable experiences in the executive search business for a number of years. It still amazes me that the role of top-flight executive search professionals has not been fully understood by the business world and its advisors. My hope is that this book will throw some clarity on what the business is all about.

I feel particularly fortunate to have decided to go into this business when I was in my thirties. It has provided me, and, I hope, hundreds of colleagues, a fascinating insight into what life is all about. Every search assignment is different and represents a new challenge. Being in the search business is like reading an exciting novel with a list of fascinating characters, and so far I've been unable to put that novel down.

The best part about being in the search business is that it doesn't feel like work. It is a pure pleasure. The profession has a long way to go in improving its overall position in the business world; however, thanks to many of the pioneers in the business, it has definitely arrived as a highly regarded, worthwhile, if not critical, professional activity

PREFACE

that is essential to the growth and success of healthy businesses. No serious board of directors should choose a top executive without the advice of a good executive recruiter.

There are three things that make a business successful: a good idea, capital, and the people who make it all happen. In my view, it is the last ingredient that makes a critical difference and is the key to ultimate success. It is also the hardest to find.

X

5/3/12 4:50 PM

ACKNOWLEDGMENTS

This book could not have been written without the caring assistance and hard work of several people, particularly, my daughter, Chase Reynolds Ewald, who did considerable editing of the book, and my fabulous assistant, Kathy D'Aloisio, without whose professional touch this book might not have happened. I am also appreciative of Carol E. Curtis, who spent many months preparing and researching much of the flavor of this work.

CHAPTER 1

LIFE BEGINS AT 62

The 1989 annual report of Russell Reynolds Associates (RRA) featured a beautiful photograph of the famous ancient Greek sculpture *Winged Victory of Samothrace* on its cover. The picture, on the twentieth anniversary of the founding of my (now former) firm, was chosen because of its suggestion of victory, success, and confidence in the future. By that point, the firm had really arrived. With 21 offices worldwide and a staff numbering more than 500, we were enjoying the most productive years in our history.

Four years after that annual report was published, I retired from the firm with enthusiasm and confidence in the future. I had made up my mind two years earlier that I wanted to create a new life for myself. I felt that my persona, name, and actual being had been so engrained in my business that it was time for me to free myself up and reacquaint myself with my family and friends and other interests. Nevertheless, actually leaving the Park Avenue headquarters of a firm that bears my name—to which I had devoted virtually all my time and energy for more than two decades—was emotionally difficult and took some serious readjusting. Negotiating this transition was a lesson in embracing major change, with good advice from lots of well-meaning people, and using the change as a building block to the next stage of my career.

The 1980s had been highly productive years at RRA. We had grown at something like a compound rate of 23 percent a year for 20 years. Each year seemed to mark a new major milestone. In 1983, new assignments exceeded 1,000 annually for the first time. In 1984, we opened offices in Singapore and Sidney, followed by Frankfurt, Melbourne, and Tokyo in 1986. In 1987, the year we opened the Minneapolis–St. Paul office, I promoted Hobson Brown, Jr.—at the time, one of my closest business friends and a popular and productive executive in the firm—to the position of president and chief operating officer.

It all made for a pretty picture, but within six years, I would walk out the door of the firm I founded, unsure of my next step and still reeling from the rapid chain of events that had led to my departure. I wondered how long it would take for the door to close. Now it has.

RUMBLINGS AND INSURRECTION

Despite appearances, discontent had been brewing at RRA for some time. In fact, the history of executive search is filled with examples of creative destruction, with firms growing out of other firms as a result of key employee defections. Early headhunting operations, housed within management consulting firms like Booz Allen and accounting firms like Price Waterhouse, spawned early recruiters such as William Clark, which in turn led to RRA.

Still, I confess I was surprised that RRA was not immune from this trend, despite the fact that I had a reputation for hiring talented, well-educated employees with entrepreneurial ambitions—and outsized egos—of their own.

The first intimations of discontent came from David Norman, a highly impressive, dynamic, and successful recruiter based in London. By the 1980s, our London office (established in 1972) had built a reputation as the most consistently successful executive recruiting firm in the United Kingdom. That was due to hires who were both well educated and well connected. Norman, a graduate of Eton and Harvard Business School, took the firm in London to new heights in terms of brainpower, connections, and drive, and the office expanded commensurately. Revenues and profits were impressive.

By 1980, Norman was made managing director of the London office. That was the year we successfully recruited Ian MacGregor as the chairman of British Steel, marking the first time in the United Kingdom that a nationalized industry employed a headhunting firm to recruit its chief executive.

But Norman was restless, self-confident, and eager to run his own show. After prolonged conversations about

3

the firm's culture, he left RRA in 1982 to form executive search firm Norman Resources Ltd. A year later, in what British writer Stephanie Jones described as a "mass defection," three other RRA London consultants, Norman Broadbent, Julian Sainty, and James Hervey-Bathurst, departed to join Norman. Taking along four additional RRA employees, they formed London-based executive search firm Norman Broadbent International.

RRA's London operation survived relatively intact, thanks in large part to our expertise in financial services, my own specialty and a lucrative niche for any executive recruiting firm in London. We kept chugging along. In fact, after a few short years, the London office's profits exceeded its revenue at the time of Norman's departure.

HIGDON AND JOYS

The next tremor was closer to home. It came from Henry Higdon and David Joys, key RRA employees who went off on their own and, in doing so, generated considerable worries.

Higdon joined RRA in May 1971, making an immediate impact at age 29. He established our Houston office, then moved to Los Angeles in 1980 to grow the West Coast operation. Shortly after, Higdon opened a San Francisco office and was soon wired into the key players in the business world up and down the California coast.

Higdon had been gone from headquarters for nearly a decade when we agreed he would return to New York, which he had been visiting intermittently for staff meetings. But Higdon by his own account was not altogether happy with what he saw. Joys had recently returned from running our highly successful London office and was also frustrated.

"Things had changed in the firm," Higdon says now, reflecting on why he became dissatisfied. "They'd go around the table at staff meetings and say what new business calls we've made. It wasn't focused as much on quality of searches, execution, getting the job done. And the worst thing I saw [was] that the associates, the younger people in the office, started reporting to office managers who were practice leaders as the firm grew, and developed these specialized practices. Instead of pleasing the clients, the associates started pleasing the bosses. . . . It was not as entrepreneurial."

NONCOMPETES

Another aspect of the firm that had changed since Higdon's departure for the West Coast was my decision to institute noncompete agreements. Associates were prohibited from doing business at another search firm with clients they had worked with at RRA. Higdon did not approve.

The year was 1986, and RRA was going strong, still gaining momentum every year and growing exponentially. Before coming back to New York, Higdon leveled with me, "Russ, we like LA, and if I started my own firm I could do it right here in LA. I'm current; I know the market; I know the clients; I know the people. If I come back, I want to know what your thinking is, and what my future at the firm is." Higdon also wanted his noncompete agreement to be waived.

Sensing storm clouds ahead, I invited Higdon out to my home on Clapboard Ridge Road in Greenwich for a meeting over dinner. We talked things over for six hours. Recalling the meeting today, Higdon says, "It was about what I thought about the firm; it was about me, about the future of the firm." In the end, "[Russ] agreed to waive the noncompete," says Higdon.

HIGDON, JOYS, AND MINGLE

But Higdon indicates that he was still not satisfied: "I was in charge in Houston, you know, and in charge in many ways on the West Coast and in Los Angeles. Then two other guys in the firm, David Joys and Larry Mingle, approached me, and the three of us talked." After determining that the West Coast arm of RRA had enough people to survive without them, the three agreed that they would leave the firm and start a competing company, called Higdon, Joys, and Mingle.

At the time, February 1986, RRA was coming out with a new brochure. Higdon knew he had to tell me, and he agreed to be the first person of the trio to do so. But I already had gotten wind of the defections, and when I confronted him, he was not immediately forthright with me. "Hank," I said, "I have to know what your plans are."

"Russ," he said, "don't worry. If I left the firm, I would not be in the new brochure."

In fact, Higdon had already begun to talk to investors and plan possible locations. He knew he had to break the news. Finally he did. It was a short meeting: "Thanks very much, you can leave," I said. "And you can take all of your possessions with you."

The next day, Higdon started dialing for clients. But he was careful to avoid tapping his former clients, despite his lack of a noncompete agreement. "It was very important to me to have an extremely honorable departure," he says today. Still, we did not speak for five years. (Ultimately we reconciled, and today we are close friends.)

IN THE GRAND TRADITION

At about the same time, writer John Byrne visited RRA's New York offices while researching his 1986 book *The Headhunters*. He wrote:

Those who enter [Reynolds'] 35th floor lavish Park Avenue offices in New York witness the embellishments of a true WASP establishment in the grand tradition of Morgan Stanley. . . . There is, for example, in the same room

with a Steinway piano, which no one plays, a lit oil painting of Warren Hastings that hangs on a wall between a
pair of tall gold candlesticks. . . . Reynolds' sitting room
boasts an antique drop-down writing desk with a silver inkwell. The walls are enlivened with signed letters
addressed to him from Henry Ford II, President Rea-
gan and Prince Charles. There are framed pictures, too,
including one signed by Winston Churchill, another
of Reynolds' training class at Morgan Guaranty, and
another of his 57-foot yacht *Windsong*.

The elegant impression had been carefully orchestrated. It was designed to create an aura of power, class,
and success and act as a signal to employees and visitors
alike that we had arrived, were influential, and could
make things happen in the business world.

By that time, the aura was well deserved. RRA had grown
faster over the preceding five years than any other major
search firm in the United States except Korn/Ferry, which
was roughly a leap of 25 percent a year from 1980 through
1985. By 1987, new assignments exceeded 1,600 annually.

"KILL THE KING!"

The 1990s, however, ushered in two difficult years for the
firm, as business suffered due to a recession. Corporations were more focused on layoffs than hiring, and new
searches slowed to a trickle. As we struggled in this chal-

lenging environment, two distinct groups emerged in our firm: those loyal to me and those clustering around longtime board member John C. Beck, one of the original investors in RRA, and Hobson Brown, whom I'd recently promoted to CEO.

I had brought Brown in from J.P. Morgan in 1977. A Vietnam veteran and graduate of the University of North Carolina, Brown was a hunting and fishing enthusiast who favored office decor that included 1970s-style lava lamps, a far cry from the Steinway piano, English antiques, and paintings by Winston Churchill that had become RRA trademarks. Nonetheless, I had promoted him steadily, and in 1991, Hobson Brown became CEO of the firm. He was famous for great one-liners, his sense of humor, and his lovely wife, Erwin. Unfortunately, it was an imperfect arrangement from the start. I even employed outside consultants, twice, to try to work out a successful relationship, but given our different style and personalities, that never really happened.

In hindsight, I realize that if I was an otter—sociable, enthusiastic, and relationship driven—my protégé was not. "He turned out to be a shark in otter's clothing," recalls Lee Getz, my cofounder. Tom McLane, who joined RRA in 1978 and stayed for 20 years before moving to RSR Partners, explains, "1991 and 1992 were not good years at RRA. The board and key inside people wanted to keep an eye on costs. Hob [Brown] was good at that."

In 1992 the hostile camp approached. Lee Getz and others at RRA in an effort to recruit them to join them in taking over the firm. A handful of inside managing directors and outside directors came to me and asked me to make significant cutbacks, including deep personnel cuts. I was reluctant to do that. I've always been an optimist, and I believe that you have to spend money to make money. I also believe that when there's a downturn, it usually heralds an incipient upturn. I wanted the firm to be well positioned for the upturn when it came. Leon Levy, the retired senior partner of Oppenheimer & Co., always told me that you have the best business opportunities when your competitors are focusing on a recession.

Recalls Brown, "What made Reynolds successful was the freedom to do it his way. He is an entrepreneur. He did not like the idea of cutting. I cut the budget. That was considered a hostile act. There were things that were tearing the two of us apart."

It's true. I didn't like the idea of cutting back on good people during the 1992 recession. We pruned out those not suited for the business every year anyway. But frankly I had gotten tired of the job and the constant traveling. I also liked working with my sons, which was not popular with some in the firm. But the reality is that the unrest within the firm was coinciding with a desire for change in my own life that I'd recently come to recognize. I did not want to lose my persona to the firm life and had decided it was time to move on because I wanted to be with my wife and family and grandchildren more. At the same time, I wanted to keep busy, since I don't play golf.

One day, Beck went to Brown and said the board was concerned that things were not going well. The board was going to decide whether to keep Brown or me. "I didn't have anything to do with it," Brown maintains. In December 1991, Brown as CEO called a mandatory meeting of the executive committee. I planned to inform the committee that night of my decision to retire. But the event turned out to be a surprise sixtieth birthday party for me with dozens of senior colleagues and spouses there, and so I was compelled to attend, have a few drinks, and be festive. What a shock! It was a great party at a French restaurant in the East Sixties, and it delayed my plans to retire.

Ultimately, Beck came to me and suggested that either Brown or I should go. At that point I informed the board members of my desire to shift gears. I left it to them to work out an agreement. They said I had done a great job. I was fairly compensated financially, but there was not a lot of love lost at that time.

FED TO THE LIONS

Having decided to leave, I was then asked to repay a routine prepaid bonus as part of the wave of cuts; this and other fine points were stipulated in a nonnegotiable document presented to me with no lawyer present. I was offended, but at the same time I believed in behaving like a gentleman. I didn't want to leave on a sour note, and so I did my best to chalk the unpleasantness up to a learning experience. I had told the members of the board that I wanted no accolades and wanted a seamless transition, but I did not expect them to take me literally! The agreement, however, basically was fair I thought, and I still think so.

My decision to leave wasn't readily accepted by everyone at the time. Lee Getz advised me that as the controlling stockholder (I owned around 16 percent of the firm and managed its ESOP), I should get rid of the troublemakers and quash the critics.

Jonathan Bush, a board member of RRA for over 40 years before his resignation in 2011 (he is now a member of the RSR Advisory Board), felt similarly. "Some of the younger executives got antsy over the senior partner owning so much of the firm," Bush recalls. "They chose to get together and suggested to Russ that it might be time for him to move on. They made a joint effort." He reflects, "Russ should have fired them. He could have controlled the board, but he really was intrigued with the buyout. It is a sore spot because he could have easily averted that situation." Jim Hurlock, a good friend and then chairman of the prestigious law firm White & Case, had similar and equally strong feelings.

Still, I did choose to leave, and one has to move on. After I resigned and Brown took over as chairman as well as CEO, he addressed the situation in an article he wrote for a booklet commemorating RRA's twenty-fifth anniversary in 1994. At the time, Brown was one year into his tenure as president and CEO of the firm.

"I think the changes I've instituted have not been that radical at all," he wrote. "We were the cobbler's children.

We did a lot of things as collateral duties. We did a lot of that on the back of an envelope. We needed a higher level of professionalism. We needed the skills we didn't have."

After my departure from the firm, he said, "Members of the Executive Committee have a sense of empowerment now, a sense that they're encouraged to take risks and make mistakes. Reynolds would have loved for those people to take responsibility for everything. But they didn't think that, and that's the difference."

Brown and I have different interpretations of the events leading up to my departure from RRA, but it can't be disputed that he was effective at growing the company and managing cash flow. As the economy picked up, revenues continued to increase, as did profits. Brown has now retired, and my eponymous firm continues to flourish with 39 offices and almost 1,000 people around the world, without any real shift in direction or policies. Today, RRA's principal competitors remain the other four industry leaders: Heidrick & Struggles, Korn/Ferry International, Spencer Stuart & Associates, and Egon Zehnder International.

For my own part, I found that I had overestimated my appetite for downtime and that retirement wasn't for me—at least not yet. So I took the lessons I learned and the skills I possessed—including plenty of entrepreneurial drive—and lost no time in founding a competing firm, originally The Directorship Search Group, now RSR Partners. Today our firm continues to grow, and it competes on many searches with the Big Five recruiting firms, with offices in New York, Greenwich, Cleveland, Chicago, and

Los Angeles. We recruit corporate board members and senior executives, including CEOs in human resources, financial services, the private equity industry, technology, sports management, and consumer products.

For a time after I left, I would wonder what might have happened had I stayed on at RRA as it grew to even greater heights. But there is no debating the fact that the creation of RRA (a mere $10,000 investment!), the changes it brought, and the standards it set for the industry dramatically transformed the field of executive search and gave me a great feeling of accomplishment.

The fun of building a great service firm with the help of natural leaders, including Lee Getz, Hank Higdon, David Norman, Ferd Nadherny, Clarke Murphy, Daniel Jouve, Peter Drummond-Hey, Gordie Grand, and Henry de Montebello, to name only a few, cannot be overestimated.

And so at age 62, I was free to do almost anything I wanted. What follows is the story of the best years of my life and how I achieved equilibrium in life, along with the lessons learned along the way and how anyone—from MBA candidate, to middle manager, to successful CEO—can adapt them to his or her own life and career.

CHAPTER 2

EARLY YEARS

In October 1929, less than a month after the stock market crash that brought on the Great Depression, readers of the local newspaper in bucolic and prosperous Greenwich, Connecticut, may have been astonished to learn that all was well. The *Greenwich News and Graphic* boasted on its front page that the town's Grand List of all real estate was up 25 percent from the prior year, and prophesied a "continued healthy increase."

Even as the catastrophe unfolded, news about national events remained hidden in the back pages of the paper. In mid-November, industrial stocks on the New York Stock Exchange had fallen by 50 percent, but the *News and Graphic* was unimpressed. A week before Christmas, it proclaimed, "Holiday Trade Biggest in Greenwich History."

This was the setting in which my parents, recently married Russell and Virginia Carter Reynolds, found themselves in 1930. Shortly before the marriage, my father had gone into the retail dry goods business by opening a store on the main shopping street, Greenwich Avenue. Soon after the store opened, I came into the world as Russell Seaman Reynolds, Jr., born on December 14, 1931, in Greenwich Hospital.

As I grew and the Depression unfolded, even the *News and Graphic* had to bow to reality: in 1934, along with stories about sheets of ice closing Greenwich Harbor, the paper carried articles about the Public Works Administration, the new federal agency through which many unemployed Greenwich men found temporary work.

Notwithstanding the town newspaper's head-in-the-sand position, the Great Depression affected every type of business in Greenwich, including the dry goods store my father owned and ran. Thus, by way of helping out, as I entered school, my mother opened a dress shop behind my father's store.

Still, even in the throes of the Depression, Greenwich was then, as it is now, a wonderful place to live. With its beautiful coastline and natural harbors, hardwood forests, and horse farms, Greenwich was idyllic. It had a historic downtown with classic steepled churches; it had country lanes overarched with maple trees and lined with weathered stone walls. There were many grand estates owned by wealthy New Yorkers such as the William Rockefeller family, who had relocated from New York City to the country, as well as E. J. Converse of Conyer's Farm, once a gentleman's farm, now famous for its world-class polo.

The Reynoldses, among the first founders of the town of Greenwich in the 1640s, came from farming stock— humble but well educated. My family's belief in the value of a good education had been instilled by my grandmother, also born a Reynolds, and because of it, priority was put on ensuring I received top-notch schooling.

This same grandmother, Mary Adeline Reynolds, as well as my mother, had a strong influence on me, not only because of her stalwart pursuit of education early on, but because of the resourcefulness and entrepreneurial instincts that she displayed later in her life. Eventually a successful real estate developer, in her early years she traveled to Greenwich Academy on horseback. The school was so far from the Reynolds family farm on Stanwich Road that Mary boarded during the week in downtown Greenwich and came home only on weekends.

I picture her riding down leafy lanes on the roads that are now identified by white wooden signposts with black lettering, with little fingers pointing down them. Later, in the 1920s, horses were everywhere. Fox hunting was popular, as was show jumping, and the town boasted a distinguished polo team. The scenery also featured 13 miles of waterfront property, exclusive yacht harbors, and eventually ultramanicured golf and tennis clubs, where members dressed in white were served tall glasses of iced tea by uniformed waiters.

As an adult, and after a quarter century of married life, Mary Adeline was forced to fend for herself when my grandfather John Jay Reynolds (a distant cousin) abandoned her in 1911. But after being thrust from her comfortable life in a fully staffed New York City brownstone and a country house in Greenwich, Mary Adeline did anything but play the role of the helpless victim.

Instead, she leapfrogged from operating a successful boarding house to embarking on a career as a builder, despite having no relevant experience. As described in *Loyal to the Land*, a history of my family published in 1990, in a single development named Cedar Hill, "She built large houses, mostly in the Tudor style, with steep tile roofs, brick and stucco walls, and half-timbering adorning the exteriors." She had little difficulty selling the houses for up to $80,000, a fairly princely sum in the 1920s.

Mary Adeline's success in the male-dominated world of real estate development was truly inspiring to me. It clearly required strength of character and grit, and those qualities made an impression on me. In later years, I looked back with admiration on Mary Adeline's determination and work ethic, and I've sought to emulate the self-reliance and the resolution that made her so successful. Although, unlike her, I do not carry a Bible with me for answers to business questions. I do, however, harbor the same commitment to always trying to do the right thing.

SCHOOL DAYS

My own education began in the Greenwich Public Schools. Then I continued on to the Brunswick School, a private boys' school in Greenwich. My family could not afford it, but the school needed students. Charles W. Pettengill, a prominent Greenwich lawyer who was chairman of the board at Brunswick, said to my father, "Well, what can you afford?"

Dad replied, "Oh, I don't know, maybe $500 a year, or something like that."

Pettengill replied, "Fine. We'll take Russell."

At Brunswick, I proved sociable, and dabbled in athletics. My grades must have been adequate because in my sophomore year I was fortunate to transfer to Phillips Exeter Academy in New Hampshire, one of the best preparatory schools—and one of the least expensive at the time—in the country. My mother's brother, Franklin Chase Carter, had gone there and wanted me to have the same experience.

I recall boarding the *State of Maine Express* sleeper train in Stamford to go to Exeter as one of the happiest moments of my young life. Despite my wonderful relationship with my parents, I could hardly wait to get out of the house. I felt the world was calling me, and I was in a hurry to embrace it.

When I was a senior at Exeter, I was told to visit one of the masters. "Where are you going to school?" he asked. "There's Harvard, and there's Yale, and there's Princeton, and you know some people go to places like Brown and Williams." I said, "Well, I kind of like Yale." He said, "Fine." Oh, were that the college application process for my grandchildren today!

A Higher Education

At Yale, I thrived both academically and socially, learning early how to manage my time while also discovering the fact that having interesting friends could open doors. My favorite subject was European history, and I joined in just about every extracurricular activity under the sun. I rowed on a club crew team, sang in the glee club, and joined the Fence Club, a fraternity describing itself as "a bunch of nice guys." It was the first time I ever heard the word *nice* used to describe males. I asked, "Well what does it mean?" and an older member said, "Well, you're one!" I still didn't know what it meant. But I found out, I think, maybe 40 years later—it means "genuine." As an officer of the Fence Club, I became involved in recruiting members for the fraternity. I was sort of a social animal, which sometimes got in the way of my studies.

One thing that set me apart from many of my friends at Yale was the fact that I had worked every summer from the age of 14—excellent training for the hard work of being a successful entrepreneur. There was never a country club or a tennis lesson. Instead, when I was very young, I was expected to go up to my uncle's farm in Kinderhook, New York, near Albany, and help pick apples for $10 a month. I did not admire people who didn't do anything, and so I thought it made sense.

As I got older, I not only labored in a gold mine in Alaska, but worked for an insurance company on Wall Street, toiled as a grease monkey in a Rolls-Royce garage, sold ties in a clothing store on Greenwich Avenue called Kepple and Kepple, and served as a crew member on a yacht. All throughout, I kept a shoebox full of dollar bills, counting them, trying to build a nest egg, but I was not very good at saving money.

As hard as I worked, however, as a senior at Yale I was still hard up for money—so much so that my roommate had to lend me $300 so I could finish my last year. And upon graduation, my father's sister, Edna Ferris, gave me $500 so I could lead the Yale Glee Club European tour of 1954. It was a wonderful experience, especially since I sailed home with Greenwich friends on the *Queen Elizabeth*!

The tour took us to Belgium, France, Switzerland, England, and Wales, where we performed on grand concert hall stages under the adoring gaze of local debutantes. In Lausanne, I remember sitting next to the mayor's gorgeous daughter at lunch one sunny day, when I heard a loud noise outside. It was our tour bus leaving. Strange, I thought, since everyone was still at the lunch table.

As it turned out, one of my friends had decided to give the mayor's other daughter a scenic tour of Lausanne. It was a large bus, and my friend had no experience driving one. It was a long time before the bus returned, and all the while I had visions of being sued and thrown in jail. Ultimately, they returned safely, to my everlasting relief and embarrassment.

Another funny episode during my stint as glee club president happened upon our return to the States. The group had a singing gig in Pittsburgh and was headed for a preconcert dinner party at the impressive Heinz home. I got directions, and we started up this big hill with two buses containing about 80 young men wearing white ties and tails. We arrived at a huge mansion with all the lights on and lots of cars. It seemed obvious that this was our destination, and so we stopped and everybody got out—a whole bunch of young guys, ages 20 and 21—and wandered into and around the house.

Finally, a man came up to me and said, "Can you tell me what you are doing here?" I replied, "Well, aren't you Mr. Heinz?"

"Oh, no," he said. "The Heinz house is next door." I remember it like it was yesterday, and it still makes me chuckle.

My singing exploits at Yale didn't stop with the glee club, however. Jonathan Bush, a younger brother of George H. W. Bush, who was ahead of me by one year at Yale, helped me get elected to the Whiffenpoofs, the elite singing group for Yale seniors. We performed every Monday night at Mory's (Yale's famous eating club), were in demand for campus concerts and events at the home of Yale's president, and were hired for parties and receptions. The dress for almost every performance was the same: white tie and tails, with white gloves. Between the Whiffenpoofs and my role as president of the Yale Glee Club, it's amazing that I ever got into the classroom. But during my last year at Yale, I actually had the best grades I'd ever had.

Friends to the End

Friends that I made at Exeter and Yale were to stay with me throughout my life. For instance, Donald K. "Obie" Clifford, a classmate from Exeter and then a Yale roommate (the same roommate who floated me the $300, allowing me to finish out my senior year), and I established a close bond that only grew stronger over the years. Clifford, from an old Bronxville, New York, family named Lawrence, founders of Sarah Lawrence College, went from Yale to Harvard Business School, graduated a Baker scholar, and then joined the consulting firm McKinsey & Co. He later proved instrumental not only in helping me start my executive recruiting business, but also by serving as a longtime board member of RRA and RSR Partners.

I loved my time at Yale, and it's still a huge part of my life. As an alumnus, I became class treasurer, served as a reunion chairman, and was in charge of special gifts, and currently I am class secretary-elect. I also still sing with the Whiffenpoofs and participate in glee club events.

Flying High

Whether fun-loving and social or not, most students during the years leading up to the Korean War felt it their duty to serve in the military. At Yale, I joined the Air Force ROTC program and trained one summer at Otis Air Force Base in Cape Cod.

After graduating in 1954, I joined the training program at J.P. Morgan & Co., but after just three months, I was given a leave of absence to go on active duty in the Air Force. There I served as a navigator bombardier in the Strategic Air Command (SAC), flying B-36 airplanes and working as a special weapons instructor for nuclear weapons.

The SAC had been created as a global command in 1946. After that, a group of SAC bombers were kept in the air around the clock as a deterrent to action by communist-bloc nations. Planes carrying nuclear weapons were kept on alert, and their crews had to be physically sound and carefully trained. I was accepted by this command with the rank of first lieutenant, making several trips across the Pacific Ocean as a navigator-bombardier in the select crew of over 20 B-36s.

The following year I was stationed at Mather Air Force Base in Sacramento, California, taking a special weapons course. In late 1955, I was on a blind date with two friends in San Francisco when I met University of California graduate Deborah Ann Toll. Debbie, who had attended Smith College back east for two years, was far from impressed by my eleventh-generation status in Greenwich. "That's a terrible place," she said. "People are stuffy, and I've never been comfortable there." I decided then and there that Debbie was the girl for me.

I was not sorry that, like me, Debbie did not come from considerable wealth, although the members of her family were leading citizens of Los Angeles. I didn't want to share my life with someone who'd had a lot of money, was spoiled, and had no work ethic. Some of the Greenwich girls I had escorted to balls and coming-out parties, though delightful, were quite self-centered.

Still, she was from a prominent Los Angeles family; her father, Maynard Toll, was a pioneering tax attorney whose clients included celebrities such as Walt Disney and David Selznick. He had graduated from Harvard Law School and was head of the law firm O'Melveny & Myers. Debbie's

mother was often featured in the pages of the *Los Angeles Times* for her charitable works and social activities and in her role as a board member of Occidental College.

Within weeks I had proposed, and on July 21, 1956, we were married in Los Angeles. I spent the next 18 months in El Paso, Texas, with the Air Force. When I finished my tour, I drove back with Debbie to New York in the fall of 1957 with our son Trey Reynolds, age four months, in the back seat. Initially, we lived in New York City's Stuyvesant Town before moving to Armonk, New York, where Obie Clifford's mother-in-law sold us a house on Rose Hill Drive for the grand total of $25,000.

The pretty house had one flaw that I remember all too well: It was built on a clay bank that would not absorb water—whether it rained or came out of a toilet. So there was often a large puddle on our lawn. There, our second son, Jeffrey, who had just been born in New York, joined our family. I commuted to Manhattan every day, and Debbie threw herself into the life of a young mother and the life of the community.

BACK HOME TO GREENWICH

After 18 months of interesting living in Armonk (we discovered that the man next door was absent because he was doing time in prison), we moved again, this time back to Greenwich, where well-known real estate broker Jane Newhall found us the picture-perfect home: a white house

in the woods with plenty of privacy, even if it was 30 feet from the road.

When Newhall told me I could have the house for $40,000, I recall clearly what I said next: "Jane, $35,000 is *it*. No matter how we stretch, that's all we can do." Newhall called me back a few days later and said, "Well, you have the house for $35,000 net."

I said, "What do you mean, net?" And she replied, "Well that's what the seller is going to get."

And I said, "Yeah, but I told you we can't afford anything more than 35." And she said, "There won't be a commission."

The experience made a big impression on me. It was a great example of "If you give, you get," because we were so impressed and grateful that we sent every single friend from New York to see her for the next 20 years, and they all bought houses from her.

Our daughter Chase Reynolds Ewald was born in Greenwich hospital in 1963.

AN OTTER, NOT A SHARK

By this time I was also beginning to learn where my true talents lay—and that they were not of the "win-at-any-cost" variety. In college, I was busy having a good time and loved being sociable. I don't know if you can type people by personality, but if so, I was definitely an otter. The otter is affable, friendly, trusting, fun loving, playful, quixotic, and

kind. Like the otter, I do not go for the jugular. I don't make people bleed and squirm, and I don't seek to win at any cost.

Nevertheless, I managed to float into Exeter, Yale, J.P. Morgan, and the top reaches of international executive recruiting. Could it be that so-called management experts have it wrong about the advantages of sharks versus otters? I happily consider myself living proof that they are!

CHAPTER 3

IN AND OUT OF
J.P. MORGAN

Before leaving the Air Force, I considered a military career, but decided against it in favor of business. When I was winding up my military stint, someone asked me what I wanted to do, and I explained that I planned to return to J.P. Morgan. The interviewer asked where I thought I would end up, and I modestly replied, "Probably as chairman of the board."

This burst of confidence came from a habit of running the best-case scenario, rather than the worst-case scenario, in my mind. You may know you will probably never get there, but I always figured, why settle for less? The Air Force then wrote a memo to my file that said, "Mr. Reynolds must have some very special connections, because he's going to be the chairman of the board of J.P. Morgan & Co."

The famous House of Morgan traces its roots back to London, where it was founded as a merchant banking firm by George Peabody. Junius S. Morgan became Peabody's partner in 1854, soon taking over the firm and renaming it J.S. Morgan & Co. in 1864. In the meantime, Junius's son, John Pierpont (J. P.) Morgan, established a New York sales and distribution office called J.P. Morgan & Co. in 1861.

J. P. Morgan inherited his father's businesses in 1890 and consolidated his and his father's business five years later under J.P. Morgan & Co. Going forward, Morgan played a key role in financing many of the businesses that turned the United States into an industrial power, including General Electric, U.S. Steel, and AT&T.

Morgan was instrumental in pulling a group of bankers together to stave off the 1907 financial crisis. There was much criticism, however, of the power that Morgan and his bank wielded, power derived particularly from the system of interlocking directorships that led Morgan partners to hold 72 directorships on the boards of 47 corporations; together the corporations were worth $10 billion, a princely sum at the time.

A 1912 investigation into these interrelationships led to the passage of the Federal Reserve Act of 1913 and the Clayton Antitrust Act of 1914, the latter of which ended reciprocal directorships.

There were other bumps in the bank's growth trajectory. In the wake of the 1929 crash, around the time I was born, the famous Pecora investigation demonstrated that Morgan and the men of his circle had acted improperly in disposing of the savings of working people invested with the bank. As reported in *The Tycoons* by Charles R. Morris, a history of how J. P. Morgan and others invented the "American super economy," banks at that time, including Morgan, "routinely bundled bad loans and securities on their books into mutual funds that were sold to retail investors, pumped up the funds' nominal assets with borrowed money, and engaged in deceitful trading operations to drive up their prices."

Such practices were multiplied many times on Wall Street at the time, and they were an important factor in the crash of 1929. Concludes Morris, "Whatever sense of honor such men had in dealing with each other clearly did not extend beyond their class."

But ultimately, such investigations proved little more than hiccups in the bank's remarkable growth. In 1940, J.P. Morgan & Co. was incorporated under New York State law. Two years later, the firm went public.

As I returned to Morgan in 1957, the expanding bank needed more capital and higher lending limits, and it merged with Guaranty Trust Company in 1959 to form Morgan Guaranty Trust Company of New York.

Reentering the bank at that time, I saw a place in which I felt comfortable. I had gone to Exeter and Yale, educational bastions of the establishment. Plus I already knew many of the people in the financial community. It seemed a natural place to be, an extension of the worlds with which I was already acquainted.

Although I may have had the right connections, my path at the historic bank was far from assured. My view of the institution was initially confined to the municipal bond department, where I was sent to work following completion of the standard training program. After the merger with Guaranty Trust, I was shifted to the national division and became an assistant vice president and loan officer.

Back then, the bank's services were organized by geographic territory, rather than industry. I was initially assigned to the Southeast and traveled to Tennessee, Kentucky, Mississippi, Alabama, Louisiana, Georgia, and Kentucky, calling on officers and directors of the biggest companies in the region.

I was essentially a salesperson for the bank, working to get customers to increase their loan business with Morgan. The sweet spot for me was that I met all the top people in the places I visited, experience that would come in handy later, when I started my own business.

The position opened up a new world, and I relished it. To be successful at a prestigious national bank like J.P. Morgan, you had to have more than a first-rate education; it required a gregarious personality, plus knowledge of lending and finance, proper manners, and an understanding of social conventions—all of which I had.

Also crucial to a young banker's success was his attendance at the never-ending stream of banking conventions, inevitably featuring a cast of thousands. As a young married man, I was expected to show up at most of the ones in my area, often without my wife, Debbie. So I went to my boss and said I wasn't up for many more conventions, since it kept me away from home too much.

The boss replied that the freedom to choose to take your wife happened to be open only for vice presidents. I pressed the issue until finally the bank let Debbie go along on the company expense account—a move that may ultimately have benefited the bank more, given my wife's intelligence, charm, and keen social antennae.

One snowy winter day, we drove into New York to cohost a large Morgan cocktail party at the American Bankers Association Trust Conference—a premiere industry event. As junior hosts, we worked a crowd numbering about 2,000.

As we were driving home, I asked Debbie what she thought of the party. She said, "You know, I am not really crazy about such large events, but I realize that it's good business and you have to do it." She was not in a good mood.

"Were there any people there that you liked?" I asked.

"Well, there was this one woman I really talked to a lot, and she said she didn't like these things, either."

And I said, "Do you remember her name?"

"Ann something."

"It wasn't Ann Patterson, was it?"

"Yes, that's it." It turned out that the woman was the wife of Elmore Patterson, next in line to be J.P. Morgan's chairman of the board of the bank. Was it happenstance? Definitely not. But it didn't hurt then, and it helped mightily going forward, that I had a wife who was willing if not always eager to lend a helping hand on the social front.

Two more years passed, and I became restless. I asked for another assignment and was assigned to the Midwestern banking district. While the bank called it a promotion, I was not convinced. The management explained that the desk I was being moved to had been occupied by three former presidents of the bank!

I didn't know if it was a guarantee in my case. I was covering Missouri and Iowa, states where the bank had major business with companies like Monsanto, Ralston Purina, and Anheuser Busch. In particular, I spent a great deal of time in St. Louis—and while I may have liked the city and the Midwest, I soon began asking myself if I was being paid enough for the day-to-day grind that went with the new territory.

A critical turning point came one day when I was back at headquarters and got a telephone call from none other than Elmore Patterson, who at that time was executive vice president in charge of the general banking division, a position that qualified him as my boss. "Can I see you for a minute?" he said. I went up to his well-appointed second-floor office, where large rooms were lined with pictures of old Morgan partners and a fire was burning in the fireplace. I was filled with trepidation.

"I just want you to know that you are not going to be promoted to vice president," Patterson said. I sat transfixed.

I said, "Oh." I didn't have the slightest idea what to say or do. I had never been in a situation where I felt that awkward. Finally I said, "Well, am I going to get a raise?"

"Oh yes, you're getting the maximum raise and bonus, but you are not going to be made vice president because two people are ahead of you." What Patterson was probably trying to say, I later realized, was that I needed to keep my pants on, and that while I wasn't going to make vice president this month, the prospects were bright. But Patterson didn't actually say that.

I took the news hard, especially since the person promoted in my stead had not, in my opinion, been working as hard as I had been and had gotten the job through clever politicking. I felt insulted, and the pain did not go away. Recognizing that I was ambitious, my boss made me understand that I would eventually make vice president—that I should wait, work hard, and not worry too much about the workings of what amounted to a very well-run company. While this system had its drawbacks, it led to a certain stability. The old-boy network was a reality, stuffy but useful if you happened to belong, as most CEOs did.

TURNING POINT

The insularity and complacency (and even snobbery) at Morgan continued to bother me. Casting about for alternatives, I looked to contacts from Greenwich and Yale—in particular, William H. Clark and John Isham, friends I had met through my membership in one of Yale's senior societies. They now ran an executive search firm called William H. Clark Associates in New York.

Clark had opened an account at the bank through me, and when I saw the size of the deposits that were coming in, and the names of the well-known companies that were paying the fees, I looked into the company's balance sheet and other activities and became deeply intrigued by the search business.

I was also quietly putting my hand in the job market by answering ads in publications like the *Wall Street Journal,* including one placed by Goldman Sachs, which made me an offer to cover upstate New York. After interviewing with the firm, I was offered a job for $10,000 a year more than I was getting at Morgan.

Well connected though I was, I knew my status probably was not enough to be able to bring in the Ford Motor business, or a large initial public offering, and I didn't have an MBA like many Goldman executives (although I did attend New York University's business school for two years at night). I also knew that Morgan was well on its way toward becoming a global investment bank. Weighing the comparison, I decided against Goldman.

Then Isham introduced me to textile giant Collins & Aikman, where CFO Alex Stewart expressed interest in hiring me as assistant treasurer. I went back to Isham and told him, "While I appreciate your introducing me to these people, frankly I think your business is more interesting than theirs is." With that, Isham introduced me around at William Clark, and I entered the executive search business there in 1966. My base salary was $18,500 plus bonus. A major drawing card was the easier commute: Morgan's offices were downtown at 23 Wall Street, while Clark's headquarters were on Madison Avenue, just a block from Grand Central Station.

Clark was a fellow Yale graduate who had ended up in the personnel department at accounting firm Price Water-house. That led him into executive search, where he could found a company owned by its principals in an industry that, unlike heavily regulated banks, was not regulated at all and went unrecognized by the federal bureaucracy: it was free enterprise, and it was interesting, and so I thought it would be a natural fit for me.

QUICK STUDY

I proved a quick study. After a short time with the firm, I was having lunch with Isham and a client at the New York Yacht Club, when Isham paid me a distinct compliment by saying to the client, "Russ Reynolds here knows more about the search business than the rest of us put together, and he's only been with us for six weeks!"

Clark's firm made its money the way retained executive recruiters still do: via a monthly retainer plus expenses. For example, the CFO of General Foods, David Brush, called Clark and said he needed an assistant treasurer to work in White Plains. The position paid an annual salary of $80,000, not a bad amount in those days. Clark's fee was 25 percent of the annual salary, or $20,000. The firm charged a $5,000 monthly retainer against that fee for a period of three months. If the firm found a candidate who took the job, the retainer was subtracted from the $20,000, and Clark was still owed $5,000. If the firm did not find a candidate, $15,000 was all it got, plus expenses.

Executive search firms still work in basically the same way today, except that the fee has increased from 25 percent to 33⅓ percent plus expenses. Often the total fee is negotiated. Sometimes there is also an administrative fee equal to 5 to 10 percent of the total retainer.

Clark had eight or nine partners, most of whom were not stockholders. Revenues were relatively modest. Growth came from having a steady stream of searches, so that there was always new fee revenue coming in.

I soon became one of the firm's largest revenue generators, due in part to my close relationship with Oppenheimer & Co. head Leon Levy, which I had worked diligently to bring about. Feeling I had earned the right to some additional recognition, one day I went to see Clark and said, "You know, we just got another assignment from Oppenheimer. I don't know how I can handle all the work. I would really like to be able to go to Harvard Business School and hire a bright young person to be my assistant: do the research, write the memos, smile and dial, all that stuff."

Clark replied, "If we do that for you, we have to do it for everybody else."

I said, "Not everybody else has the problem I've got, which is too much business."

I was politely rebuffed—even though I was the number one producer. "Well," he said, "any one of the other partners here would be happy to help you."

I never told Clark what I really thought—which was that if I had been doing the hiring, I would not have hired most of the other partners, because I did not think they were at a level where they could do the job that Oppenheimer demanded. In fact, I was having a hard time understanding Oppenheimer's business myself because it was so different from what I knew. I had also noticed that many people chose the recruiting business after pursuing another career—meaning they tended to be older. I held my tongue for a moment, then made another suggestion.

"I think we ought to have a brochure." Clark initially dismissed the idea as being "too promotional and not very professional." But I did not let up. While I didn't know what it would cost, I argued that a single good search would very likely pay for it. And I thought the chances of getting, at the least, one more search by executing a good brochure were extremely good.

After more arguments along the same lines, Clark finally bought into the idea and put me in charge of it. The total cost proved to be a relatively modest $6,000, and the result was the first brochure ever done by a search firm, a radical departure from the standard word-of-mouth approach at the time. As it turned out, that brochure produced a lot of business and pointed the way toward what was to be a hallmark of my style: leveraging personal con tacts with the aid of elegant, high-quality printed material, embellished with top-quality photographs and illustrations and professional writing. Such an approach went a long way toward creating an elite impression.

In all, I stayed three years with Clark, soaking up knowledge, building relationships, loving the business, and carrying out search assignments for companies such as the Bank of Montreal, General Foods, Oppenheimer & Co., White Weld, and other financial services firms. The search business was a lot of fun in those days, because the firms were much smaller and because the business was free-wheeling, minimally overseen by a group now called the Association of Executive Search Consultants, or the AESC.

I was asked to join the AESC planning committee, where the other three members—Spencer Stuart, Ward Howell, and Gardner Heidrick—also became leading names in the early years of executive recruiting.

MORE CHANGE AFOOT

By the spring and summer of 1969, I found myself hungry for a change. I had made it clear to Clark that I wanted a larger say in the management of the firm, based on the substantial contribution I was making. Clark had told me that I would be the president of the firm some day, but I didn't feel reassured. Instead I asked, "Yes, but when? And what is the job description?"

The answers to those questions were crucial, since Clark basically owned the firm. There were two other stockholders, and I wasn't one of them. Equally important, I did not get along with one of the other stockholders. I felt I might never be president.

And yet despite my restlessness during that time, I could not deny some of the wonderful benefits of being a company man. One of the perks that is hard to imagine today was the Special Car Associates. Train service from Greenwich to Grand Central was a rarefied experience for the lucky executives who rode in this private club car for commuters, run largely by members of Greenwich's exclusive Round Hill Club. They leased a private car from the New Haven Railroad that was reserved only for them. They would then drive their cars down to Fitzsimmons's garage at the corner of Railroad Avenue and Arch Street—today, the site of a Lexus dealership—where they got out, handed their keys to an attendant, then crossed the street, climbed to the train station platform, and ducked into the curtained car reserved for the business elite. Regular riders included CEOs from well-known firms such as Price Waterhouse, Citigroup, Smith Barney, Newmont Mining, and J.P. Morgan, plus famous names like Prescott Bush, Jr., Stillman Rockefeller of Citigroup, and Bob Powers, CEO of Smith Barney, and I was lucky to be among them.

We were served by a porter, who would bring ice water while we read the paper or business materials while others played bridge. Upon arrival at Grand Central, the porter would perform personal services like taking suits to be mended at Brooks Brothers.

Alas, the special treatment ended when the railroad declared bankruptcy, and then-Connecticut governor Ella Grasso decided the private car had to go. But it worked magic for me, because I became friends with many captains of industry in the Special Car, top executives who would one day become clients of Russell Reynolds Associates.

As a young businessman starting out, these perks seemed natural. My path to Exeter and Yale was straightforward. And when I moved into the rarefied world of Wall Street as an employee of J.P. Morgan, and afterward William Clark, I already knew many top people in the financial and business community. It was an extension of the world I had grown up in. What stayed with me from those early experiences was a feeling of security. But I found that with the security provided by the old-boy network also came insularity and complacency. Simply by not screwing up, I was discovering, one could inexorably advance through the ranks. For me, that predetermined path was far from enough. And thus I was about to take a right turn.

CHAPTER 4

THE BIRTH OF RUSSELL REYNOLDS ASSOCIATES

After three years with Clark, the notion of striking out on my own had taken hold of me. I never seriously considered the possibility that I wouldn't be successful. I felt I had everything going for me. I was good at the business. I was young. My biggest problem was that I may have been a little too young. What's more, I looked even younger. (At 35, I had trouble buying liquor in a store, even with two young sons in tow!) While youthful looks are the sort of problem many people would like to have, they weren't to my advantage in the executive search business. Interacting with and impressing senior executives was critical, and so I found that I had to work extra hard to be taken seriously.

A CERTAIN STYLE

Whatever credibility points I may have lost to my young age, I made up for in style. I knew that I possessed a certain manner when it came to business—a chumminess crossed with a courtliness—and it helped me mightily. As a case in point, when I was starting the business, I recall that I received a call from a prominent British businessman who ran one of England's largest merchant banks, asking me to undertake a search. He said he wanted the best candidate for the job, and then he told me he had already decided who it was.

"We don't work as messengers," I replied. "We only do full searches."

"Well, of course," came the reply. "But if you ended up recommending Mr. X, that would be very helpful."

I was engaged to do a full search and ultimately did end up recommending Mr. X, as he was the best candidate for the position. Mr. X told them he would accept the offer, which he did. The businessman and I had an understanding; probably the Englishman and Mr. X had an understanding, too. It was all very gentlemanly, and very fraternal.

SETTING UP THE FIRM

Although the members of my family were initially less than thrilled to see me go into a business that did not have a superior reputation, thankfully I did eventually win their support. Still, other unexpected obstacles cropped up at home in the early days of Russell Reynolds Associates (RRA). My wife, Debbie, a gifted athlete and a competitive tennis player, had been having serious back pain and was told she needed surgery. Meanwhile, my father was seriously ill and in the hospital to have his esophagus removed. Being the only child, I was his sole caretaker, while I was also tending to Debbie and our young kids at home. Still, I was presumptuous enough to believe that the firm would succeed.

As it turns out, this period of crisis led me to one of the most critical business decisions I've ever made. I knew that I was in over my head and that I needed a partner in order to spread the risk and to avoid the responsibility of sole proprietorship. I said to Debbie, "I've got to find somebody who's going to make the business succeed." And she said, "What about Lee Getz?"

At the time, Getz was working as a vice president at Manufacturers Hanover Bank. I called him up and said, "Would you have a little time to chat with me about an idea that I've got?"

It was the summer of 1969. We met in the city and drove out to Greenwich together in my aging Oldsmobile 98 convertible. As we drove from the fringes of Manhattan and along the Henry Hudson Parkway to Greenwich, I laid out my idea for a new search firm.

Getz was not immediately convinced. His wife, Connie, in particular, had spoken to people who were not sure that executive recruiting was a respectable occupation. In fact,

45

her father, George Hinman, a prominent Nelson Rocke-feller Republican and a senior partner in his Binghamton, NY, law firm and corporate director of several companies, was asking hard questions.

So on Labor Day weekend, with both my wife and father in the hospital, I left Greenwich to fly up to Hinman's summer home on Martha's Vineyard to make the most important sales call of my career.

"Tell me about this executive recruiting firm you're planning," Hinman said over a glass of iced tea. "You are going to start a firm, and you actually believe my son-in-law ought to be in on it?"

Although polite, Hinman seemed incredulous.

I pressed on, noting how bright I felt the opportunities were, and how the business was totally unregulated and unnoticed by Congress. It was the focus of no federal legislation, and moreover had a low cost of entry and an easy bailout. I said, "If it doesn't work out, so what? You're still alive and haven't burned a lot of bridges."

I also said that I thought it could be a lot of fun and that the two of us—Getz and I—could really build something.

Hinman said little, apparently unconvinced. I returned to Greenwich downcast.

A few days later, I reported back to Getz on the trip: "Lee, I don't know how the meeting with George Hinman went. I tried, but he asked a lot of tough questions, and I must admit he made some good points."

Getz laughed. "Well," he replied, "now you've really created a mess, because now he wants to invest in it."

THE ORIGINAL INVESTORS

Besides Hinman, the small group of original investors included Getz; the family of Yale roommate Donald Clifford; the family of John Beck; Louis Marx, a private investor; and Dan Lufkin of Donaldson, Lufkin and Jenrette. I formed a board of directors in part because the original investors were stockholders, and so I felt they should also be directors. The board also included the firm's attorney, Richard C. Pugh of Cleary Gottleib, as well as Jonathan Bush, a younger brother of George H. W. Bush, a longstanding friend of both Lee's and mine from our Greenwich and Yale days.

As for my new partner, Getz got a healthy chunk of equity—37½ percent—and I got 62½ percent, with each of us contributing a corresponding share of $10,000. I put in $6,250, and Getz, $3,750.

It was considered extremely unusual at the time for a firm like this to have an outside board of directors, since they had very little to do with running the firm. But I had a different strategy: I felt the board would be very good for the firm's image and would create an aura of stability and solidarity. I also thought that having a prominent, well-connected inside group to give advice and counsel would be very constructive in building and running the business.

The move was prescient. While the board only met two times a year, my father-in-law, Maynard Toll, ultimately joined along with John H. Loudon, the chairman of oil industry giant Royal Dutch Shell, who at the time was also head of the international advisory boards at Chase and Ford.

Loudon became one of my best directors and also a close friend of my family—we spent several vacations together sailing in the Caribbean and around the Greek islands on his Benetti yacht, *Ivara*.

The advisors then became business developers. I particularly recall one meeting in George Hinman's offices at Rockefeller Center when Hinman said, "Your little firm seems to be perking along. Isn't there some way I could be helpful?"

I replied, "Well, like what?"

Said Hinman, "Well, I don't want to be pushy, but if I wrote a letter to a few of my friends and enclosed your brochure, telling them what a great bunch of guys you were, it might be helpful."

To my great delight, Hinman had with him a yellow legal pad with the names of his friends on it, 100 of the most prominent businesspeople in the country at the time, people like Henry Ford and David Rockefeller. Hinman knew them all. I couldn't believe my luck. "What a class act," I thought. And it was all the more admirable because I hadn't asked him for the favor.

Years later, when I asked John Loudon to join the board, Loudon said, "Why would you want me on your board? Is it to help develop business?"

"Oh, no!" I replied. "For your advice, friendship, and counsel, to make sure we don't make mistakes and to help keep us out of trouble."

Loudon accepted and remained a valuable member for almost 20 years.

I felt that the risk of setting up the board this way was minimal, because I retained control of the firm via ownership of over half the stock. While the original investors each owned stock in the beginning, in 1973 we repurchased the shares from all the outside stockholders. After that, they were just paid fees, plus perks that included elaborate trips abroad with spouses to places like Hong Kong, Paris, and Madrid, where they were (literally, in some cases) feted royally. We were entertained by the king of Spain, ambassadors, and presidents.

THE FIRST 10 YEARS

I founded Russell Reynolds Associates, Inc., on October 2, 1969, with the stated objective of "providing a fresh and more thorough approach to the already crowded and growing field of executive search." To announce the new firm, we sent 2,000 embossed announcement cards to business friends and associates and arranged to have all phone calls transferred to the offices of law firm Cleary,

49

EARLY SEARCH APPARATUS

When I was setting up shop in the 1960s, searches were done in a rather primitive fashion. Rods were inserted into cards with holes punched into them. These cards were punched according to certain codes: whether the person was an engineer, accountant, metallurgist, or whatever, whether he spoke French or Spanish, and so on.

Wires ran through the holes in the cards, and cards would be pulled up containing the characteristics of the people the firm was seeking to fulfill a search. I recall that it actually worked well.

Files of all the candidates were kept in hard copy, housed in a machine called a Lektriever, which was a large automated filing device that revolved on a belt. It weighed so much that the company had to have the floor reinforced to prevent it from falling through to the office below! I'm still waiting for the Smithsonian's call, requesting we donate the relic to the museum's Office Life Antiquities Wing!

Gottlieb, Steen and Hamilton, since at that time RRA had no permanent offices!

Getz and I each had a base salary: I was paid $40,000 and Getz, as executive vice president, got $35,000.

FIRM RULES

RRA had a handful of strict rules as it started out. First, we would not bring any clients to the firm from William Clark, to avoid any accusations of unfair competition. Second, we did not solicit business. This move directly emulated the modus operandi of law firms, with the idea that momentum from existing business would lead to new business. Third, we did not advertise, and fourth, clients paid a retainer in advance.

The way it worked was that the firm would usually be paid a retainer for three months, plus an increment if the candidate's compensation turned out to be higher than anticipated. The total fee typically was 25 percent of the first year's compensation. We charge a retainer against the anticipated fee. So the retainer on a $100,000 annual salary would be $25,000, plus 25 percent of anything over $100,000. We did, however, raise the ante from the get-go by charging $33\frac{1}{3}$ percent, rather than the standard 25 percent. This move required a lot of optimism, but ultimately it paid off.

GATHERING STEAM

One of the first clients to walk in the door was chicken giant Frank Purdue. While the relationship was not destined for the long term, the new firm did business with Purdue for the next several years.

Soon after RRA was set up, I was contacted by Talton Kendrick, a Yale Whiffenpoof and friend, who wanted to know if RRA had any interest in acquiring the search firm he had set up in Connecticut. We ended up buying it, which largely meant taking over the lease on a very old automatic typewriter along with Kendrick himself, who was very helpful during the five years he was in New York with the firm.

Another early hire was an old friend from the bank, Jack Goodwin, who called me up after he retired from J.P. Morgan at age 65. "You know, I think I'd be a damn good headhunter," I recall him saying. I thought, "My God, what are we going to do with this guy?" Still, we hired him, albeit at an exceedingly low salary to start.

Goodwin had, after all, been calling on prime Midwestern companies for 30 years at J.P. Morgan. He knew the territory, and he was a gentleman to boot. As it turned out, Goodwin stayed with RRA as a good producer for the next 13 years. Then, when he was 78 and I finally persuaded him to retire, I threw Goodwin a retirement party at the beautiful River Club in New York.

We gave him a silver tray, a large check, and a dinner dance. He took the money and went on a one-month trip to Asia with his wife, Polly. And when the elderly Goodwin got back, he called me up and said, "I want you to be the first person to know that I'm a vice president of Korn/Ferry International!"

Even in those days, when age discrimination suits were rare, no one could accuse the executive recruiting industry of being less than welcoming to mature executives, whether they were 65 or 78. It was a fine place to establish a second career after retiring from a successful first one.

EARLY CORPORATE CULTURE

Given the fact that in its early years executive search didn't quite pass the smell test, I knew it was critical from the start to try to change that perception and to create a reputation for quality. We wanted to be the best, and that means you have the best people, the best office, the best staff, the best equipment. Quality attracts quality.

I felt appearances were an important part of this. The address, the choice of an office, and the ambience of the office are all very important ingredients in the life of a company. As soon as we could afford it, we took office space on Park Avenue and decorated it accordingly.

Big, well-known companies served as an early model. Understated, elegant office decor was a must, as were high-quality brochures filled with headshots and glossy, well-illustrated annual reports. Early on, the firm's offices featured a Steinway piano in the reception area and a painting by Winston Churchill in one of the interviewing rooms. I tended to hire recruiting professionals who were fit and had a strong handshake.

Don Kendall, who was the retired chairman of PepsiCo and, at the time, chairman of the Search Committee of Pan American Airways, came in one day during his search for a CEO for PanAm. "Your fees are too high!" Kendall said. "I can tell by looking at the decor here. It's too expensive."

"Don, you should talk," I replied. "You've got $125 million in sculptures and a lot of modern art right outside your window. Pepsi's offices and property are the most extravagant and lavish in the history of American business, and you know it. We're just trying to keep up with you." Kendall roared with laughter—he was amused, not offended, by the remark. We are still friends.

Another early client was Ben Heineman, chairman of the Nominating Committee of the Board of the First National Bank of Chicago and also chairman of Northwest Industries, where he had been a great success. RRA was tapped to do a search for First National to recruit the new CEO of the bank. The successful candidate was a man named Barry Sullivan, who had been an executive vice president at Chase.

When RRA undertook the assignment, Heineman told me, "You cannot overcommunicate with me." He gave me his home phone number, his wife's name, and every bit of contact information possible, including the phone number of his yacht.

I recall that the search was an extremely exciting and exhilarating experience. One day, I was leaving Heineman's office with him, and he was carrying three large bags loaded with papers. I said to him, "Ben, can I help you carry those bags?" Ben said, "Thanks, but when I need your help, I'll know it's time to retire."

We then rode in Heineman's corporate limo to the place where private planes are kept at the Chicago airport and boarded a De Havilland jet. When we were comfortably seated in the back of the plane, the steward on board immediately produced two stiff bourbons on the rocks, as we had just completed a long day of work in the city. Just as we were raising the glasses to our lips, the nose gear on the plane collapsed, leaving the jet at an angle of 30 degrees facing the ground.

Undeterred by this development, Heineman asked the captain of the plane quite volubly to give him a full report on what happened to the landing gear. Then, upon exiting the plane, he calmly walked over to the hangar, where he had another De Havilland jet waiting in case anything went wrong.

I learned two lessons that day: One is that you cannot overcommunicate with people. The other is that you should always have a spare jet handy.

A Dynamic Duo

As other search assignments began rolling in, Getz and I established a routine. Getz would drop by my house on Clapboard Ridge Road in Greenwich every Saturday morning, where we would spend about four hours going over the week's activities. As the firm grew, we had once-a-year meetings, upgraded to the Coral Beach Club in Bermuda, where discussions were held and decisions made on compensation, bonuses, profit-sharing plans, and other company matters. The two of us ran the firm as partners, with the understanding that I was chief executive.

I believed when I started the firm that it was better to own a little bit of a lot than a lot of nothing. In other words, if RRA was just a one-person firm, doing, say, a mere $1 million a year, it's not much consolation that you are the sole owner.

I also believed that I needed Getz as a partner, because I was confident that the firm would do well, and I did not want to bear all the responsibility. I felt it was important to be able to have a personal life: to spend time with my family, to ski, sail, and play tennis, to go to Europe, and also to build the firm. I felt that if I had a trusted equity partner with a large minority stake in the company, I would be free to spread my wings and open offices in other parts of the world, secure in the knowledge that there was somebody back home with a real sense of responsibility, who cared about the future of the business as much as I did. I think it worked.

There was also a very important social aspect to our partnership. Our wives were close friends and had both gone to Smith College. We all lived in Greenwich. And our fathers-in-law had gone to Harvard Law School together, which was important in bringing us together. Not surprisingly, we also belonged to many of the same clubs, including the Round Hill Club in Greenwich, the Links Club and

THE BIRTH OF RUSSELL REYNOLDS ASSOCIATES

the River Club in New York, the Mill Reef Club in Antigua, and others.

Getz, with his measure of caution and financial acumen, was an effective check on my risk taking. He gave good advice, worked effectively with others, and successfully took on many of the important financial services searches.

Even so, our dynamic teamwork wasn't always enough to produce a winning candidate. In a profile that became part of an oral history project at Columbia University, Getz recalls being contacted by the nominating committee of one of the world's leading banks. The committee had a high regard for the bank's chairman, who, sadly, had cancer. The chairman wanted the president he had selected to be his successor, but the president failed to impress the outside directors.

It became Getz's assignment to work with the board and bring in a slate of outside candidates. Getz met with the stricken chairman, who was very helpful. But right from the beginning, the chairman said, "To be candid, you and I are working at cross-purposes. I really want my man, but these other people don't."

The process continued, and the candidate pool was whittled down to one. The board planned to meet the next day to ratify the candidate it had selected, with Getz's help. Then out of the blue, Getz received a call from the chairman: "Thanks so much for your help," he said. "As it works out, I don't think we are going to be requiring your services any longer. I went to the doctor today and

i-xii-001-202_Reynolds.indd 57   5/3/12 4:50 PM received the finest news. Not only is my cancer in remission, but they have eliminated the tumor altogether. My doctor tells me I'm in perfect health, so there's no need for an outside person to come in."

Getz immediately contacted the search committee head, who was not surprised: "Oh, that's typical," he said. "We've been outfoxed by him."

Four months later the chairman died, and his choice, the internal candidate, took over as chairman.

DOUBLING DOWN

A critical point in the firm's development came at the end of 1970, when revenues were $500,000, with a gross profit margin of a generous 30 percent. By that time, there were 13 employees, and RRA had handled 72 assignments. At the end of the year, the country plunged into a recession. I was worried about what to do, because even though business had been brisk until that point, the last few months were terrible. As of December 1970, the firm had not received a single new assignment in six weeks.

I took a chance, said a prayer, and decided not only to pay the customary annual bonuses, but also to start a profit-sharing plan and to move RRA's offices to a more luxurious space at 245 Park Avenue, formerly occupied by Cresup, McCormick & Paget, a well-known consulting firm at the time.

Fourteen months into the new venture, I had doubled down. Some people—call them turtles—would have pulled into their shells and waited until business got better before doing these things. But it was the end of a tax year, and at the end of a tax year you want to do certain things to minimize taxes and maximize compensation. I flat out decided that life goes on and the sun will come up tomorrow. So I made these decisions based on a sense of history, faith, and hope, and turned out to be right.

Sure enough, in January 1971, the phones started to ring again, and by the end of the year, business had almost doubled. It was smooth sailing from there on out. And we began to set our sights beyond New York.

GOING ABROAD

In 1972, after three years in operation, revenues topped the $2 million mark. New assignments were running in excess of 100 annually, and I decided it was time to expand. Reasoning that London was second only to New York as a financial capital (those roles are now perhaps reversed), and knowing that financial clients were a crucial part of the business, I decided that having a presence in London would give the firm a cachet with investment and commercial bankers.

Easing in with a small office on Curzon Street, as a subtenant of client Oppenheimer & Co., the firm soon moved to Knightsbridge and then to One Mount Street on Berkeley Square, eventually occupying four floors of the building.

Even though our firm was the last of the major firms (Heidrick & Struggles, Spencer Stuart, Korn/Ferry International, and RRA) to enter the London market, it was "far and away the most successful," says Stephanie Jones, author of *The Headhunting Business.* Jones attributes this partly to our expertise in financial services, an area where demand was reaching unprecedented heights.

"The elitist image that Reynolds himself so carefully nurtured has been successfully transplanted in British soil," she said. "Reynolds has achieved the highest fee income in the British market through adapting to the British way of doing things while retaining an American approach to marketing and business development. It has achieved the former as effectively as Spencer Stuart, and the latter as profitably as Korn/Ferry, to produce a combination more successful than either."

As in the United States, RRA in London operated with a high sense of style; we even employed a full-time chauffeur who piloted a stately gray Jaguar. We held one grand and glorious dinner at Apsley House, a magnificent mansion at the end of Hyde Park. There were 120 guests, including clients and their spouses, with candelabra five feet high gracing the tables. The head of Salomon Brothers gave a toast to RRA, calling it "The best firm in England, without which Salomon Brothers would never have achieved its level of greatness in the U.K."

Promotional activities, including a corporate tent at Wimbeldon, frequent pheasant shoots, and an annual summer reception at St. James Park, paid off in spades for the London office, which became a prototype for other offices around the world.

WESTWARD EXPANSION

The same year, I hired Ferdinand Nadherny, a star football player at Yale and an experienced Boyden recruiter, to establish an immediate strong presence for the firm in Chicago.

After graduating from Yale and Harvard Business School, Nadherny went to work for Cabot Corp. and later was tapped as executive secretary of the U.S. Office of Economic Opportunity. He entered the search business via Boyden Associates, Inc., with some trepidation: "The biggest hurdle to get over," he later wrote, "was the poor image the industry seemed to have."

Nadherny was a strong leader and enjoyed helping to remake the image of the executive recruiting industry, and he liked the opportunity to control his career, which he felt was greater in executive recruiting than in other fields of business: "In the executive recruiting business," Nadherny says, "if you are really good at it and build a power base and reputation with your clients, you're in control. That was the entire rationale behind my decision [to enter the search business]."

Nadherny gave me a call one day and said he was going to be in New York and wanted to talk to me about some thoughts he had. He then pointed out that RRA had nobody in the Midwest. "Why don't you consider opening an office in Chicago?" Nadherny asked.

At the time, RRA was known mainly for financial searches, while Nadherny's background was more industrial. From his base in Chicago, he could cover the Midwest, the industrial heartland. So it seemed to Nadherny that it made sense for us to open an office in Chicago to complement the one in New York.

I jumped at the idea. In about 20 minutes, we reached an agreement to open the office under Nadherny's leadership. We agreed on his salary, and we shook hands. We never had a business plan, did no market research, and never put anything much in writing.

Nadherny went back to Chicago to set up the office. "There was just me [in Chicago]," he recalls. I found a little space. I found a secretary and decided to experiment. I went to the University of Chicago business school for interns."

The Chicago office took off. We gave Nadherny quite a bit of autonomy, which he thrived on. From day one, he felt as though he was running his own business. He recalls just one bad experience, when Lee Getz called from New York near Christmastime to make sure everyone was still in the office. "That didn't sit well with me at all," Nadherny recalls. "I told him, 'Hey, you guys don't have to do any checking. Just mind your own ways there in the East. We'll carry on here.'"

I took the hint. After that, I would go out infrequently to visit clients, but mostly, Nadherny was on his own. Early clients included Gould Inc., International Harvester (now Navistar International Corp.), First National Bank of Chicago, and other large corporations. The business grew, and before long, the office employed 50 people and was a star outpost of the firm.

Much of the success was due to Nadherny's skill—and also to the fact that I knew enough to let him exercise it. Central to Nadherny's strategy was his interest in developing new hires after they had established industry expertise elsewhere. "Many people join us after working in a given industry," he says. "They've got the industry knowledge that it takes to provide a high level of client service, but probably have little experience at recruiting itself. Recruiting isn't a business you can start doing just like that. There are a lot of fine points and subtleties. You have to do the work, with the help of an experienced recruiter who can teach you the ropes."

Unlike me, who always had a long list of candidates in my head, Nadherny felt that the most difficult part of the search process is identifying the outstanding candidates. "That takes a lot of hard work," he recalls. "Calling a lot of sources and talking with associates who have met the person and getting their viewpoints."

Also difficult for him, he says, is writing the candidate letter—the document describing the candidate and explaining what makes the candidate tick and detailing his or her job history. What he really enjoyed instead, he says—and what he was exceedingly good at—was "building a team of people and seeing the team thrive and grow."

With our complementary qualities, we clicked from the start. "Russ was a real entrepreneur," Nadherny recalls. "Quality means a great deal to him: a quality business, quality people."

I gladly return the praise. Part of having good values is that if you are working for somebody and you feel an obligation to tell the person something he or she may not want to hear, you tell the person anyway, though you may risk getting fired. There were many nights I stayed up, anguishing over things Nadherny had said. But most of the time, he was right.

Of course, it didn't hurt that the Chicago office turned into the firm's cash cow: solid, steady, predictable, and an unqualified success. It soon became the leading search firm in the Midwest, and Nadherny was rewarded later with the presidency of RRA, following the retirement of Lee Getz.

A WAKE-UP CALL

Still, the firm's path west was not without its pitfalls. In the mid-1970s, with searches climbing to 250 per year, we decided to open an office in Los Angeles. First located in the Arco Tower, the office moved to the Bank of America building. Initially managed by E. Pendleton James (who came out of the Nixon White House) and later Hank Higdon, the West Coast outpost had problems from the start. It never made a great deal of money, in part, I believe, because of the nature of the search business there. There are numerous contingent search firms in Los Angeles, but not many corporate headquarters, making competition for clients particularly keen.

The main impediment, though, was that RRA was not able to establish a beachhead in the entertainment business, which is the lifeblood of Los Angeles. The disastrous and short MCA search (detailed below) was not followed by many redeeming victories, with the result that Los Angeles—unlike the other offices—continued to limp along on disappointing results.

As alluded to above, one of my biggest recruiting disasters actually happened in Los Angeles, when I was handed what I viewed as the most exciting search of my career to date: I was asked by Taft Schreiber, a vice president of MCA, to find a vice president of marketing for MCA, the powerful Los Angeles–based entertainment company, then headed by Lew Wasserman.

I went about this search and found a man I considered an "absolutely incredible individual," Alvin Achenbaum. Achenbaum said to me, "OK, so why would I be interested in this job? What is the future?"

And I replied, "Well, you'd come in as VP Marketing, but you never know where it could lead. You could even be president of the company someday."

Two days later I got a call from Hong Kong: "Russ, this is Taft Schreiber. We are canceling the assignment. You told the man we were looking for a president of the company. Mr. Wasserman is president of the company."

"I did not tell Mr. Achenbaum you were looking for a president of the company, Taft. I told him it could lead to that."

"You were not authorized to tell him that."

"Well, I know, but life being what it is, why tell the guy the job is limited?"

Schreiber was not mollified: "That is our job, to make that decision, not yours. You're fired."

I lost the client and haven't heard from MCA since. It was a bitter wake-up call for me that taught me to be extremely careful not to overpromise when making a pitch to a client. It also taught me to always be discreet.

A KEY CONQUISTADOR

It was one of my most prized internal recruits, Hank Higdon, who eventually led us south. I had initially approached Higdon, who had also gone to Yale, where he had been captain of the football team, and who lived in Greenwich when I was starting RRA.

At the time, Higdon was selling insurance with Massachusetts Mutual Life Insurance Co., which he joined after Yale and a stint in the Marine Corps reserves. I said I was calling about life insurance advice. It was not too complicated, and in the middle of our insurance discussion, I asked him if he would be interested in joining me from day one in starting the new firm.

Higdon initially was not interested at all, but he didn't want to discourage me from buying insurance, and so we finished the discussion. I invited Higdon to lunch with me and Lee Getz at the Yale Club. Higdon said thanks but no thanks, and that was that—except that Higdon was happy to have signed our firm up as an insurance client.

We stayed in touch, and Higdon, who worked with many financial services organizations, said later he kept hearing about how well RRA was doing.

Still, Higdon recalls that he was put off by the reputation of the search business at that time: "It [the industry] was totally embryonic. It was basically a bunch of people who were agents—some would say parasites—mostly working on a contingency basis. . . . It had these surreptitious, evil connotations, and it was a slippery, sort of dark business. *Shady* was the best word for it. It was the guy in the trench coat behind the potted palms."

I approached Higdon again two years later. By this time, "the firm was at the end of the runway, and I saw it lift off and gain altitude," recalls Higdon. "I was pretty impressed, and more receptive." So in May 1971, Higdon joined RRA as the fourth associate.

The big difference at that time, Higdon recalls, was a contingent versus a retained firm. (A contingent firm was paid a fee if it found a candidate the client hired. A retained firm like RRA was paid for a certain time whether the search firm found a candidate the client hired or not.)

Higdon was 29, a decade younger than I, and he clearly looked up to me as the new boss: "Russ was extremely energetic and had an incredible sense of urgency about everything," he recalls. "He was full of ideas and was a masterful salesman."

He also liked the fact that I didn't take myself too seriously, right down to my license plate, "HEADS" (a takeoff on *headhunters*, the semipejorative nickname for executive search consultants at the time).

It was a big help, too, that I entered a business that was not full of talent, high-quality firms, or real competitors. "Other people in the business were not necessarily well educated and would not have been successful in other businesses," Higdon recalls.

I aimed to change that by hiring well-educated young people with talent, ability, energy, and ambition. And in doing so, we helped create a thriving, quality-driven industry.

"More than any one person alive today," says Higdon, "Russ Reynolds is responsible for the maturation and professionalization of the executive search profession. Why? Because he built a great firm in a unique way, hiring the best people, and enabling people who had been successful in other businesses to become successful in the search business too."

As Higdon saw it then, my timing was fortuitous: "The demand for talent was going to highly outstrip the supply.

I made the call that Russ was going to be one of the leaders. That was a great call for me."

SOUTHERN EXPOSURE

It was at one of our regular staff meetings, at the Sky Club, where the subject of having a presence in Paris came up. Said Higdon, "Wait a minute. This is 1976, and we have a gap here, a major gap. Geographically, we are still not in the Southwestern U.S., and industrywise, we have nothing in the oil and gas business."

At the time, the Sun Belt was growing by leaps and bounds, thanks in large part to the skyrocketing price of oil, dating from the Arab oil embargo three years earlier. "We should be in Houston before we are in Paris," Higdon said. He recalls that he said this after a few glasses of wine, finishing with, "Not that we shouldn't be in Paris."

But the lid was off. "You know, Hank, that's a great idea," I replied. "But who's going to do it?"

He said, "Well, I'll consider it." And the meeting went on.

The next day I followed up: "Hank, I'd like to send you down to Houston for a year or two to get it going, and then you could come back."

Higdon had not yet broached the subject with his wife, an only child who had never done much traveling outside of her Connecticut hometown. But he finally persuaded her, even though she was eight months pregnant when the move took place.

Higdon made a great success of the Houston office. While the plan was for him to be there for two years, he stayed for four, attracting many of the biggest names in the oil and gas business as clients, along with local banks and money management firms.

BUSINESS DEVELOPMENT

As the business revved up, the firm became known for its first-class business strategy, all the more so because the search business at the time did not have a reputation for hiring top people or for being particularly professional.

I set out to change that image. The philosophy of RRA has always been that if you do a good job, you'll get more business than if you do a lousy job. It doesn't matter how good a salesperson you are; you won't get more business. So the emphasis has always been on executing assignments.

Direct mail also played a key role. One day, after mailing a handsome new brochure, I recall someone in the office asking Lee Getz how many had been sent out.

"Oh, quite a few," Getz replied.

"How many?"

"More than 500."

Actually, the number was closer to 5,000. We used the shotgun approach. It's a kind of overkill, but one good assignment means a lot. So the brochure is important, the letterhead is important, the location of the offices is very important, and then hiring people who know a few people is important. All these things add up to a successful business.

I also used entertaining as a business development tool, including receptions, cocktail parties, dinners at my Greenwich house, and parties in the office. There were numerous anniversary get-togethers; and whenever a new office opened, there would be a large reception.

Clients flowed in. By 1973, RRA was getting business from Lazard Freres, Morgan Stanley, J.P. Morgan, IBM, and General Foods. The new business was emanating primarily from financial vice presidents of the companies and—to a lesser extent—human resources departments. Getz and I had both worked in the banking industry, and we knew how to work a crowd, albeit in a dignified way.

Every Monday night, the firm would have a staff meeting, after which we invited CEOs of prospective client companies to dinner at the Yale Club, the New York Racquet Club, or other suitable place. That was how people really bonded in the firm.

REFINING THE STRATEGY

It was during this time that I refined my strategy of doing a search. After identifying the best candidates for a search in my head, I would pick up the phone and call the person I considered the best candidate. If that person was not interested, he or she would recommend somebody who was likely to be equally good. You want to make sure you do not lower your standards in terms of the people you talk to, because it is a complete waste of time. I've heard recruiters say, "Oh, I called a hundred people on that search, and I couldn't get anybody interested." My reaction is that they called a hundred of the wrong people. Or they're just not any good at the business.

I measured my success as a recruiter by the length of time on the phone it took me to determine whether someone would be any good at the job, and then how long it took me to persuade the person to come to my office for a meeting.

Only in rare instances would I go and visit a prospect. A good recruiter gets the other person to do it, and you've got to get the prospects salivating on the other end of the phone without getting them so excited that they will become furious if they don't get the job.

Ultimately, I learned that the recruiter is a judge. He or she listens to what the candidate says, listens to what the boss says, and then decides whether to recommend the person or not.

"IT'S ALL PEOPLE"

The qualities that are essential to successful high-level recruiting were discussed by RRA board member A. D. Hart in a book prepared for RRA's twenty-fifth anniversary celebration. Hart, Obie Clifford's brother-in-law, who joined the firm in 1970 and stayed for over a quarter of a century, said that I brought a sense of urgency to the business: "We had an internal goal, and that was to introduce three qualified candidates to a client in the first month of the assignment. That got the ball into the client's court and got them to focus on the search so that we could complete it rapidly."

The firm often identified potential candidates by talking with people who had knowledge of the specific industry the client was in. We would call people we identified to see if they were personally interested. If not, we would ask for recommendations. In the early days, there was not a lot of research available, and so staffers shared information. We had dinner staff meetings on Monday nights and talked business. Then, after getting home, we made more calls to gather as much information as we could on a company and the people in its industry.

Besides the team spirit, Hart felt that leadership was critical in the firm's early success. "The person who is a good recruiter and good at recruiting other people to the office provides the leadership and inspiration to move the office forward," he said. "What's important in this business is to manage the environment—you don't need to manage the people. If you have to manage the people, they shouldn't be here. If you are successful, you can maximize your earning power because it's all people." I believe Hart's wisdom still rings true today.

CHAPTER 5

EXECUTIVE SEARCH
GROWS UP

As my firm entered its second decade and momentum began to build in earnest, the business of executive search was facing an identity crisis. Despite corporate America's increasing reliance on outside search firms to fill top positions, the business itself was still viewed with suspicion.

When Lee Getz left Manufacturers Hanover to join me as my partner, he was debriefed by the bank's chairman, Jeff McNeill. McNeill gave Getz many reasons why he considered his decision a mistake. "The most poignant one," Getz recalls, "centered on one term: 'steegma,' as he pronounced it. 'There's a stigma associated with that industry,' McNeill told me. 'They're not very good people.'"

A. D. Hart, one of Russell Reynolds Associates' (RRA) first associates and a longtime member of the firm's board, saw it this way: "Most of the search firms were populated by older people who were fired or retired—lots of gray hair. We were the young people in the search business. Russ Reynolds, to his credit, thought this was a great career opportunity for young people; that the clients wanted to hire people who were our vintage, not people who were 60."

And in fact, almost anyone who recalls the state of executive search in the 1950s and 1960s had the same impression. "It was a little suspect," recalls Jonathan Bush. "It had a pejorative connotation."

Longtime RRA board member John C. Beck says that when I entered the business in the 1960s, he thought the industry's standards were so soft that somebody with drive and ideas could in fact take advantage of an industry opportunity. Traditionally, people who were attracted to the industry were those who were between jobs, and at that time, the work of the industry reflected that.

Beck, a Harvard Business School graduate, also recalls that the business school considered the search business "a group of parasites who were kept at bay or entertained by the corporations that used them."

D. Ronald Daniel, a former managing director (CEO) of McKinsey & Co., viewed it this way: "We see what we do as a profession and not a business." On the other hand, he added, "Executive recruiting was basically a business." Times have changed. Daniel's son David is currently the highly regarded CEO of Spencer Stuart & Associates.

THE FIRST STAGE: STRUGGLING TO EMERGE

Part of that reputation dates from what might be called the first stage of executive search, its earliest days under practitioners like Thorndike Deland. Deland, who may or may not have graduated from high school, started his career as a professional magician. He then found work as a manager with a clothing manufacturer in Baltimore, and in 1920 he became the head of the "executive placement bureau" for a group called the Retail Research Association.

In 1926, Deland opened his own firm, focusing on placing merchandise managers and retail buyers. This was very likely the first retained executive search firm. Deland charged a client $200 to do a search. If he succeeded in placing a candidate, Deland picked up 5 percent of the candidate's first year salary minus the $200 retainer.

His modus operandi made up in energy what it lacked in class. A bit of a huckster, Deland traveled around the country selling his services wherever he could. He was noted for giving speeches on subjects such as "What the Store Expects of Display Men" and for writing articles titled, for example, "Do You Beg, Borrow or Steal Your Executives?"

Following Deland's lead, the industry basically treaded water until the years following World War II. Experienced executives were hard to find in the war-starved ranks of many companies. There was little time to hire and train a whole new group of employees, so the only solution was to take them away from other firms. There were also new products fueling new corporations, including computers and synthetic fibers.

Companies hoping to enter these areas needed skilled managers who were at a higher level than the retail buyers that Deland was good at placing. The fact that there was a demand from companies for such executives, as opposed to the placement of executives who needed jobs, marked a new role for executive recruiting. Before the war, the customary way for an executive to find work was through an employment agency. But these firms, aside from the smattering of retained firms like Deland's, were mostly working for the candidate.

THE SECOND STAGE: A HOME IN MANAGEMENT CONSULTING

By contrast, executive search firms that formed after the war were working for the client. As events conspired to create a need for companies dedicated to finding higher-level talent, management consulting firms like Booz, Allen & Hamilton and McKinsey & Co. would take on an assignment and wind up urging management changes or, frequently, additions. Thus executive recruiting became a logical expansion of their consulting practices, and many founded separate departments to help clients implement the consulting firms' recommendations.

The emergence of executive search via management consulting constitutes a second stage in the formation of the business. Many of today's largest and best-known search firms date to this time. Felicitously, the spin-offs usually emulated the rigorous tenets and highly ethical behavior of the consulting firms from which they sprang.

Jack Handy, who worked for McKinsey before the war, left the firm in 1944 to open up his own firm as an executive recruiter and management consultant. In the mid-1950s, Handy began to use computers in his search work, and he is believed to be the first recruiter who did so, using them to track candidates and sources.

Meanwhile, Sidney Boyden, who worked with Deland during his long career in personnel with Montgomery Ward, left Booz Allen in 1946 to try executive search on his own.

Using a network of sources dating from his years at Montgomery Ward and Booz Allen, Boyden cultivated bankers, lawyers, and trade association executives who could recommend him for other assignments. Unlike Deland, who charged a retainer, Boyden initially worked on a contingency basis, meaning he would only get a fee of 10 percent of a candidate's annual salary if he found a candidate who was actually hired by the client. That policy eventually changed.

Boyden's firm was one of the first to become international. Other, smaller firms, such as Battalia Winston, were founded at this time and are still going strong.

At about the time my firm was gaining momentum, a handful of these headhunting firms were breaking away to become leaders. In her book *The Headhunting Business,* Stephanie Jones calls the original Big Four headhunting firms "the search industry's equivalents of the Seven Sisters of the oil world." As mentioned earlier in the book, they were Heidrick & Struggles, Spencer Stuart, Korn/ Ferry International, and RRA. With the exception of me with my banking background, these companies emerged from the management consulting business. All four are thriving today.

HEIDRICK & STRUGGLES

Heidrick & Struggles was founded in 1953 by Gardner Heidrick and John Struggles, Booz Allen veterans who set up shop in Chicago's financial district. Each partner put up $2,500 to capitalize the business. They hired Spencer Stuart, who left a year later to start his own firm, also in Chicago, which de facto had become the birthplace of retained executive search. The firm's first client was West Virginia Coal & Coke Corp., which was seeking a general manager for its retail operation, at an annual salary of $13,500. Struggles conducted the successful search himself.

Many of the firm's placements during its early years were in management and marketing. While the company prospered, its operations picked up considerably after the arrival of Gerard Roche in 1963.

Heidrick hired Roche not only for his intelligence and aggressiveness, but also for his charm and engaging personality. A natural-born salesman, he easily persuaded rising young executives to change jobs and loyalties at a moment's notice. In those days, the offer of a $5,000 to $10,000 raise enticed many executives to accept a new job even though their old job was just as promising.

By 1978, the company's board of directors was convinced that Roche should be appointed chief executive. Yet even after this appointment, Roche continued to carry a full search load for years.

At the beginning of the 1980s, Roche was poised to personally place some of the major talents in the corporate world, including Thomas Vanderslice, who was convinced to leave General Electric in order to head GTE; Edward Hennessy, who jumped from his position at United Technologies to assume the top job at Allied Corporation; and Robert Frederick, a GE employee persuaded to become president of RCA.

In 1980, the company placed approximately 600 high-level executives, but by 1982, that figure had fallen to 500. Roche was forced to reduce his staff from 100 to 82, putting the brakes on Roche's strategy for expansion. With these setbacks, RRA surpassed Heidrick & Struggles both in revenues and in ranking within the industry.

Heidrick bounced back during the late 1990s, expanding its client base to over 3,100 by the end of 1998. Most significant, however, was the company's decision to go public in 1998, with a public offering in 1999. The firm also emphasized strategic acquisitions, including the purchase of Fenwick Partners, Inc., an executive search firm based in Boston; Mulder & Partners GmbH, the largest executive search firm in Germany; and Redelinghuys & Partners, an executive search firm based in Capetown and Johannesburg, South Africa.

Today, the firm remains one of the largest and best global recruiting companies, with 350 headhunters spanning 70 offices in 35 countries.

SPENCER STUART

Spencer R. Stuart, another Booz Allen alumnus, briefly worked at Heidrick & Struggles before opening the doors of his Chicago firm in 1956. His first assignment was international: he was asked to find a managing director to run a U.S.-based pharmaceutical company's operations in Caracas, Venezuela.

The job successfully completed, Stuart discovered that much of his time was spent on international searches, and so he immediately set up offices in Zurich and Mexico City. By 1958, the firm had established a thriving international practice, the first American firm to do so. By the 1960s, the firm had expanded to 28 countries. When he sold out in 1973, Stuart was wealthy enough to retire in luxury, with homes in Vermont, Palm Springs, Lake Tahoe, and Dallas.

Today, Spencer Stuart remains one of the world's leading private executive search consulting firms. Its clients range across industries, from the world's largest companies to medium-size businesses and entrepreneurial start-ups. The firm operates 51 offices in 27 countries. In 2010, Spencer Stuart conducted more than 4,000 assignments around the world, using a team of more than 300 consultants. Tom Neff, its famous CEO recruiter, has kept the firm in the highest levels of search activity.

KORN/FERRY

Lester Korn and Richard Ferry emerged from the Big Eight accounting firm Peat Marwick, Mitchell, where they were both partners in the 1960s. In 1969, considering their prospects there limited, the pair organized what they called an "employment agency," so as not to ruffle competitive feathers at Peat Marwick.

Korn and Ferry each put in $5,000, opened up an office in Los Angeles, and were soon Korn/Ferry International, an executive recruiting firm on the make. With a sharp eye for public relations, the two were soon grinding out press-worthy reports.

Within three years, Korn/Ferry employed 42 search professionals and was on its way toward becoming a public company. In 1972, the firm sold just over 25 percent of itself to outsiders, raising just under $1 million—a pittance by today's standards, but enough at the time to make Korn and Ferry wealthy men. They later went private but did another successful IPO years later.

By 1979, Korn/Ferry had become the world's largest executive recruiting firm, with an annual growth rate of nearly 30 percent. Today, the firm operates 80 offices in 40 countries. Services have expanded from executive recruiting to include leadership development programs, succession planning, and recruitment outsourcing.

Korn/Ferry remains the number one U.S.-based executive search firm in revenues, ahead of Heidrick & Struggles, Spencer Stuart, and RRA.

MARKETING BLITZ

As these firms were establishing a beachhead at the top of the business world, the industry as a whole was growing rapidly in the United States and overseas. A landmark occurred in 1959, when the Association of Executive Search Consultants (AESC) was founded as the main trade association of retained executive search.

According to the AESC's fiftieth anniversary publication, *Executive Search at 50*, issued in 2009, the industry experienced a sea of change in the late 1960s, at about the time RRA was born. In a dramatic departure from the industry's traditional low-profile approach, Korn/Ferry International began to aggressively market itself. Lester Korn and Richard Ferry both believed strongly in public relations and marketing and courted the press with newsworthy research reports.

Following their lead, Heidrick & Struggles hired Oscar Beveridge, who directed public relations at Booz Allen, to get the firm on the map. Beveridge created the firm's first brochure, along with a series of executive profiles.

84

Journalists began to follow the industry more closely, and executives on both sides of the Atlantic found themselves on magazine covers. In October 1978, *Fortune* magazine devoted its cover to the story "The Headhunters Are After You." CEO searches by Spencer Stuart's Tom Neff, Heidrick & Struggles's Gerry Roche, and me and my associates for companies like IBM, Coca-Cola, Walt Disney, and J.P. Morgan got strong media coverage.

As some of the bigger firms began to issue public offerings, public relations and media attention became staples of the industry. Today most of the top firms routinely have PR firms and international PR staff that issue promotional releases to attract media coverage.

TWO CLEAN SUITS

There are at least two factors that make the executive search business one of the most attractive on the planet: the cost of entry is low, and there is virtually no regulation. "The business is such that you don't need a lot of capital," John Beck explains. "You need a calling card, an answering service, two clean suits, and a sufficient pedigree so that you can make your first cold call."

As mentioned above, another plus is lack of regulation. At a time when the financial crisis of 2008 has spurred fitful reregulation of the financial services industry and increasing calls for government regulation of business generally, executive recruiting remains largely untouched by

Washington. There is no grassroots movement to regulate executive search commensurate with, for example, calls to regulate hedge funds. That may be because it is a fraction of the size of the hedge fund industry, but it is also because its practitioners are for the most part educated, knowledgeable, and highly sophisticated professionals who operate under the radar at the top levels of American business.

THE THIRD STAGE: GOING GLOBAL

An additional opportunity for search firms was the spread of American multinational corporations overseas. The 1950s and 1960s was a renaissance period for the development of the U.S.-based multinational corporation, and these companies needed managers to staff overseas outposts.

The early creation of a New York–London axis has been a feature of many firms, including Russell Reynolds. RRA went global with the establishment of a London office in 1972. That followed a pattern: early on in its life, executive search became an international business. Today's search assignments may easily be commissioned in London by an Indian company seeking executives based in Paris, Shanghai, or New York.

In the 1980s, when Stephanie Jones was writing her book about executive search, she asked Roddy Gow of our London office to comment on the global growth of headhunting. Gow said that search firms at the time were significantly differentiated by the extent of their international network. The largest of these have extensive international coverage, he pointed out, while most large firms have offices in the main three financial hubs: New York, London, and Tokyo.

And since the majority of high-level recruiting projects call for the recruiter to find the best possible candidate, such searches are necessarily more international than domestic, more global than regional: "The recruiter in Singapore must be prepared to work closely with, and support, colleagues in Sydney or San Francisco if asked to do so, and this global capability in research and execution must be offered as a complete service to the client."

A more recent development is a dramatic rise in demand from emerging markets. Today, many search firms have offices in China, India, and Russia, as well as in smaller markets such as Poland, Turkey, Romania, the Ukraine, and the United Arab Emirates. Following economic growth patterns, industry market shares have changed to favor the Asian-Pacific and Latin American regions at the expense of North America and Europe.

Despite the vicissitudes of executive search, it is likely that the underlying trends of globalization and a talent shortage will persist, which bodes well for the continued worldwide reach of the industry. As the AESC points out, the globalization of the search business has led to an increasingly worldwide distribution of demand for top management talent.

STRUCTURE AND FEES

As it has evolved, executive search still consists of two basic models: retained search and contingency search. Retained search firms are customarily paid a fee equal to one-third of the candidate's annual salary when the search is completed and a candidate is hired. There is an up-front retainer paid in installments. This retainer counts against the final fee, but it is kept by the firm in any case.

Contingency search firms receive their fee at the conclusion of the search process. If no candidate is hired, then no fee is paid. For obvious reasons, executive search consultants greatly prefer the retained search model, and it has become the standard for virtually all the top search firms. The main industry trade association, the Association of Executive Search Consultants, serves only retained firms.

Normally the candidates are not actively seeking a new job. It is the job of the search consultant to approach the individuals with a view to luring them from their current company and placing them in another, often a competitor, at a higher level.

The service is paid for by the client company or organization, not by the candidate. Potential job candidates are identified, qualified, and presented to the client by the executive search firm based upon fit with a written or verbal job specification developed in conjunction with the client.

Assessing the degree of potential fit of the candidate with the job specification is a key activity for the search firm, since a common reason for a search consultant to be engaged by a client company is to save the time and effort involved with identifying, qualifying, and reviewing potential candidates for specific leadership positions.

Despite the inroads made by technology, it is still not unusual for a potential candidate to be identified by the search firm via a phone call. Often the call is the result of a recommendation from someone inside the existing network of the search firm. Top search firms work hard at cultivating and continually updating their network of contacts, so that when a search assignment is awarded, they will be ready to start recruiting potential candidates right away.

Another way to identify potential candidates is to target people in specific companies who appear to fit the job profile. Some of the best candidate referrals come from people who could be candidates for the job themselves but may not be interested at the time.

While contingency firms offer a service with no money up front, they will often only work on those searches that can be executed quickly, and they may not have the time to focus on high-quality candidates. Another option is to hire one firm and give it an "exclusive contingency" arrangement so that the money is still paid at the end of the search, but only one firm is working on the search. This gives the firm the benefit of time to focus on quality while protecting the hiring manager from being flooded with résumés. At any rate, a retained search brings a degree of professionalism sought by upper-level candidates.

FEES

When it comes to fees, the fundamentals are still the same. The fee structure has remained the same for 30 years: one-third of a candidate's annual salary. In the event that the firm does not find a suitable candidate, it is customary to reinitiate a new search at no additional cost to the client.

While the fundamentals may not have changed much, the amounts clearly have. When I was starting my firm, the CFO of General Foods in White Plains, New York, called and said he needed an assistant treasurer. The salary was $80,000, then a generous amount. The fee was 25 percent of the annual salary, or $20,000. RRA charged a $5,000-per-month retainer for three months, plus expenses. If we failed to find someone General Foods hired, the $15,000 retainer would be all that was paid, plus expenses. However, if a candidate was located who was ultimately hired, the fee would be $20,000, or 25 percent of the annual salary, again plus expenses, minus the $15,000 retainer. The idea is to have a steady stream of searches, since the primary way a firm can grow is by doing more business.

Today, the per-search amounts have grown much larger, due in large part to the skyrocketing of executive pay. A boutique firm like RSR Partners earns an average search fee of $120,000, or six times what it was in 1969, plus an administrative fee that can easily total $6,000 to $12,000. The fee is really 33 percent plus another 3 percent.

Henry Higdon recalls that when he joined RRA in 1971, his hardest job was to convince clients that a retainer, as opposed to a contingency fee, was the way to go. "We would spend half of the first meeting convincing the client to give us a retainer," he says. If he succeeded in that, Higdon says his typical retainer might have been about $4,500 for three months, paid at $1,500 a month.

Today at age 69, Higdon is managing partner of Higdon Braddock Matthews LLC in New York City, a boutique search firm that focuses on asset management firms, including hedge funds, mutual funds, and investment banks.

While the $33\frac{1}{3}$ rule still applies, he says that his clients increasingly ask for a flat fee or a cap in cases where compensation runs more than $500,000—which it frequently does, especially in the high-paying financial services area. Still, who's complaining? Even with a flat fee, a single search can easily pull in more than a recruiter used to earn in an entire year.

THE FOURTH STAGE:
FROM BUSINESS TO PROFESSION

As the search industry gained traction as a global business, it was also earning the kind of respect that had been absent earlier. One reason: a good candidate can add significant value to an organization. In one case cited by my friend Obie Clifford, after a large multinational company announced publicly that it was hiring a well-known executive for a senior position, the company's market value increased by several billion dollars in a single day. That is an immediate, quantitative measure of the value recruiting can bring to companies.

However, another crucial reason that executive search gained respect is the set of standards and values ushered in by me and my firm as well as other firms. In addition to insisting on quality people, the best office, the best staff, and the best equipment, I decided from the first that we would emulate the better law firms, which never solicit business. We would rely on word-of-mouth to bring us clients, and we would emphasize professionally executed searches and first-rate candidates as a way to grow the firm.

Validating that growth was the rapid expansion of office space at home and abroad, starting with Chicago and London. By November 1979, RRA revenues exceeded $13 million, and there were nine offices, the newest in Washington, D.C. The firm concluded work on 425 assignments that year, including CEOs, college presidents, corporate directors, heads of research, a chief drilling engineer, German-speaking Arabs, and executives in scores of diverse disciplines.

As our firm was on the cusp of landing its most prized assignment (recruiting Ian MacGregor as the chairman of British Steel), my partner Lee Getz described it this way in a letter to clients: "Our philosophy is that recruiting is an art, not a science. It is our only business. We work on a retainer basis, and never represent individuals seeking employment. Our sole objective is to provide rapid, intelligent, and relevant input on important staffing requirements of our clients. We find that this is, in itself, an adequately challenging objective."

RRA had arrived, and so had the profession of executive recruiting.

CHAPTER 6

TAKING ON THE ESTABLISHMENT— AND JOINING IT

In 1980, at the relatively ripe age of 67, Sir Ian Mac-Gregor had recently retired as chairman and CEO of Amax, Inc., but was still serving as a partner of investment bank Lazard Freres & Co. Meanwhile the British government, owner of nationalized British Steel Corp., found itself in a fix. The company had been losing more than $2 million per day, and British Steel sorely needed to be turned around.

Casting around for a new chairman and CEO, the government broke with precedent and asked the London office of Russell Reynolds Associates (RRA) to take on the search. It was the first time in the United Kingdom that an executive search firm had been called in to find a new boss for a nationalized industry. Part of the reason for the selection was no doubt the firm's premier position in the fledgling British search market.

Another reason we landed this plum assignment was David M. Norman, the then-managing director of our London office. Norman was a graduate of Eton, McGill University, and Harvard Business School with first-rate connections in Europe as well as the United States. Thus it wasn't surprising that Sir Peter Carey, then permanent secretary to the Department of Trade, looked to Norman to find a new CEO for the ailing company.

The impact of this assignment on the development of our firm—and on headhunting in Britain—is hard to overestimate. More than 100 candidates from Europe, North America, South Africa, and Australia were interviewed over a period of 10 months. Norman worked so hard on the search that when it was completed, he had to take a week of vacation just to recover from that one assignment. He traveled all over the world to nail down MacGregor and negotiate the terms of his pay package.

Part of the difficulty in the assignment was having to persuade MacGregor to accept the salary, which, relative to what he was making in the private sector, was extremely low at approximately $110,000 a year. But Lazard Freres would receive payments tangentially that could total as much as $4.1 million over the next five years to make up for his loss, which could ultimately benefit MacGregor.

The deal touched off a major outcry in Parliament, with members describing the payment to Lazard variously as "monstrous," "farcical," and "disgraceful." Still, the deal was consummated, and along with it came official recognition of executive search as an acceptable way to recruit top-level executives in the United Kingdom. I never really knew what MacGregor's arrangement with Lazard was.

While MacGregor never succeeded in making British Steel profitable, he did reduce its losses—and apparently impressed Prime Minister Margaret Thatcher enough so that she tapped him to run the government's National Coal Board after his tenure at British Steel.

For me and for our firm, the assignment was a victory on all counts. As reported in *The Headhunting Business*, "Assignments such as this . . . made an important contribution to Russell Reynolds' global earnings, and especially to the growing personal wealth of Reynolds himself."

I was feeling my oats. As I told the Columbia University Oral History Project in 1994, "I was like a kid being let out of some boring Latin course and sent to recess in a playground with a sandbox and gym equipment. We were just swinging all over the place. We had the best time, and revenues and the profits kept increasing."

Later, of course, when reality set in, the firm ultimately became numbers oriented and indeed numbers driven. But not in 1980. In those days we weren't thinking about numbers. We just had faith in each other and faith in the future and talked and loved the business. The numbers took care of themselves.

Nevertheless, the numbers were highly respectable. In 1981, coming off the British Steel assignment, profits of our privately held firm ranged from $100,000 to $300,000 a month. It was again time to expand.

HONG KONG AND OTHER ASIAN-PACIFIC COUNTRIES

After checking out Tokyo and concluding that the market there was not particularly congenial at the time, I flew to Hong Kong and consulted with John Wong, a colleague from my days at J.P. Morgan, about opening an office there. In 1981, the prospects were bright that the mainland would open up and that Hong Kong would be at the center of the action.

Again, great personal connections led to great business connections. While I was in Hong Kong, George Doubleday, who was running Pan American Airways' operations there, threw a party for RRA and invited Paul Chang, then head of Spencer Stuart's Hong Kong operation. We went to the Happy Valley Race Course and the Country Club and played tennis and squash at the Hong Kong Club and the American Club.

Ultimately I found that in Hong Kong taxes were low, the people were hardworking, and the culture was English and operated under a familiar legal system. All these factors made it very appealing, and so I decided to open RRA's first Asian-Pacific office there. To run it, I settled on Andrew Choa, who was born in Hong Kong, had a background in private banking at Citibank in New York, and had been educated at Harvard Business School. Choa's wife, France, interviewed me personally to make sure I was a suitable partner for her husband. (She remains a great friend.) It didn't take long before Hong Kong became one of the nerve centers of the firm.

Other Asian offices followed in Singapore (1984) and Tokyo (1986). The office in Singapore was unique in that it was staffed and run almost entirely by professional women. To open the operation there, I tapped Jane Kingsley, who, prior to Singapore, had also worked in the Middle East for Citibank, then joined RRA's London office, and then moved to Hong Kong as the office's number two executive. Plus, the offices were pink! It was this neat little jewel of a boutique in downtown Singapore. While not a big producer, the office did well serving clients in Asia and the Middle East. "The Middle East was a big boom area," Kingsley recalled, "so all of the banks had either branches in the area or Middle East departments of one kind or other. And so you'd start with those. It was quite a close-knit community, so all the bankers tended to know who covered the Middle East. You did it just as we do today—by sourcing heavily. We would send 150 letters out to people who we knew meant something in the Middle East and hope something would come back."

We found that the business world in the Middle East was also almost exclusively male dominated at the time. Said Kingsley, "There were no women candidates—no *successful* women candidates. It's not a female place. It's very odd. The only reason I did well was because the recruiting business was unknown, and they did business with us because they'd known John McCarthy [an expert Arabist who ran RRA's Mideast practice out of London] for many years in different guises. He had lived in the Middle East. He spoke fluent Arabic. He'd lived in Beirut for 10 years. So he had enormous trust and credibility on a personal level with a lot of people."

Despite the challenges of the Middle East's unique business landscape, Kingsley's and McCarthy's expertise made the Mideast recruiting practice a great success, and placing candidates in the region became a specialty for the firm.

PARIS

In March 1977, RRA opened its Paris office, at 4 Place de la Concorde. There was nothing pedestrian about the location: RRA took over Morgan Stanley's former office on the second floor of the building, directly over world-famous Maxim's Restaurant.

Heading the office required a skilled person with plenty of style. Initially I placed a New York associate, Michael Tappan, in the office, sending him to Berlitz to learn French. While the office held some wonderful receptions, Tappan soon left and was replaced by a Frenchman, Daniel Jouve, a Chase banker and former head of the *Nouvelle Economiste*, a French business magazine. Jouve was also president of the Harvard Business School Club of Paris.

He brought French character and personality to the operation, combined with American business training. In 1979, he was joined by Henry de Montebello, an American of French descent and a Harvard graduate who had served in Vietnam.

De Montebello knew nothing about recruiting when he received a call out of the blue from RRA associate Jane Kingsley. She said RRA had opened an office in Paris and needed "an American with a 'French hat,' or vice versa." Would de Montebello be interested?

"My first reaction," he recalls, "was, 'My Lord, do I want to be a used car salesman?' I had no concept of what executive search was."

De Montebello asked around, and—surprise—his friends advised him to take the job. "You know, you'd be perfect," said one, "because of your empathy for people, your ability to deal with people, and you can talk about any subject even if you don't know anything about it."

"At first, I was furious," de Montebello says. "Then I accepted the job."

Doing business in Paris in the early days was an "educational process" for the client, de Montebello says: "Sometimes people walking into Russell Reynolds Associates acted as if they were walking into a bordello. They didn't want to be seen." In Europe, clients were prone to thinking they could do it on their own. They thought they didn't need executive search because they already knew everybody, recalls de Montebello.

Still, his family lived in France, and his name opened doors. "There's no doubt the name helped, but only to a small extent," he says. "It certainly helps to know people, but that is only one of twenty things that is important. . . . Elitism in no way replaces the need to remain humble, hungry, and service-oriented." The Paris office did well—helped by receptions and promotional events expertly orchestrated by Jouve and de Montebello.

FURTHER EXPANSION

Other offices opened in rapid succession. In 1981, in addition to Hong Kong, RRA established operations in Boston, Dallas, and Madrid. An outpost in Sydney opened in 1984, and Frankfurt came on board in 1985.

In Germany, RRA encountered a formidable competitor in Egon Zehnder International. Zehnder, from Switzerland, attended the University of Zurich, where he earned a BA in classics and a PhD in law before graduating from Harvard Business School in 1956. He was originally lured into the business by Spencer Stuart in 1959, and then he left to start his own business five years later.

By 1980, Zehnder laid claim to being the first professional consultant in Europe specializing exclusively in executive search. He worked his way into the European market until, by the 1980s, he had a lock on much of the German-speaking search business. Today his eponymous firm still thrives, with 370 consultants operating from 63 offices in 37 countries.

Thanks in large part to Zehnder, RRA, although successful, was not able to crack the top in the German market and stayed well behind Zehnder, Spencer Stuart, and others.

GROWING PAINS

Expanding internationally can pose social and cultural challenges even for the most skilled international sophisticates. Take RRA's experience with Gerardo Seeliger, a charismatic Spaniard I recruited for a job at Bankers Trust. I later recruited him again, this time to open the RRA office in Madrid. We became fast friends.

But Seeliger was a job-hopper. After five years in Madrid, he left to join a client firm, Adidas, the global sportswear company. It wasn't long before he said he wanted to return. I put him in charge of the office in Los Angeles. Seeliger had other ideas, however, and soon left to start his own firm in Barcelona called Seeliger Conde.

Before leaving Madrid, the colorful Seeliger arranged a board meeting that included a reception at the magnificent palace of King Juan Carlos. Gerardo even arranged for me to have an audience with the king, because "I want you to know 'my King.'" Seeliger—a great promoter and a showman—left quite an impression on me when he arranged that meeting. Any executive who can arrange for his boss to have an audience with the king of his country is bound to leave something of a positive impression. I happen to think Seeliger is terrific.

Bolstered by earlier successes in London and Chicago, RRA continued its worldwide expansion spree that saw more than a dozen offices open between 1979 and 1989, including Washington, D.C., in 1979; San Francisco in 1980; Boston, Dallas, and Madrid in 1981; Melbourne and Tokyo in 1986; Minneapolis–St. Paul in 1987; and Atlanta and Milan in 1989.

Some were more successful than others. Minneapolis–St. Paul operated as a satellite of Chicago, and Barcelona as a satellite of Madrid—that is, these offices were more service arms than presences on their own. Milan struggled because, while it was in the same building as the American Embassy, business was slow in coming. The solution was to scale down headquarters and put someone else in charge. I closed Cleveland when I learned of some improprieties in that office.

Through it all, though, major assignments poured in. In 1980, we recruited Barry F. Sullivan as chairman and CEO of First Chicago Corp.; in 1981, we began a lucrative relationship with AT&T; in 1982, Walt Disney tapped RRA to recruit a vice president for the Disney Channel; and in 1983, RRA recruited Sir Colin W. Marshall to be group chief executive of British Airways, and we recruited the head of the new Hong Kong Airport Authority.

LEON LEVY

Another very important and beloved client, as well as a close friend, was Leon Levy, whose long professional investment career began in 1948 and continued into the 1990s. Levy was the senior partner and CEO of Oppenheimer and Co., the successful financial firm that created the eponymous Oppenheimer mutual funds. After leaving Oppenheimer & Co., Levy and Jack Nash founded a successful hedge fund, Odyssey Partners, in which RRA and I became participants.

In the late 1960s, I met Levy via my attempt to recruit Chuck Brunie, head of research at Oppenheimer & Co., to another job. Brunie was not interested, but he did introduce me to Levy and his partner Jack Nash, which led to a string of recruiting assignments for Oppenheimer. Levy introduced me to Oppenheimer Mutual Funds, which eventually made me a trustee for many years.

The culture of Oppenheimer was characterized by intense loyalty and total commitment and focus. Those virtues notwithstanding, Levy's focus sometimes led to absent-mindedness about other things, as at a cocktail party on Park Avenue. Levy and his wife, Shelby White, were leaving the party and asked the doorman to hail them a cab. Levy, ever polite, opened the door of the cab and got his wife seated, then went around to the other side of the cab, noticed a woman sitting on the other side, nodded, and apologized, saying, "I'm sorry. I didn't know this cab was taken."

His legendary concentration could also lead to problems. On one occasion, I was with Levy at the beautiful apartment of my friend Peter Sharp (who owned the Carlyle Hotel) to discuss a new assignment. There was a fire in the fireplace. As the discussion of the business aspects of the assignment continued, I noticed black smoke billowing out of the fireplace. After 15 or 20 minutes of near asphyxiation, I mentioned to them that the fire seemed to be burning in the living room rather than in the fireplace. Levy's concentration had been so intense that he failed to notice the smoke. Sharp didn't notice it either! Luckily, we managed to open the windows and the chimney vent before we passed out.

FIRE!

That wasn't the only occasion when fire disrupted RRA's business. In 1982, when new assignments topped 1,000 for the first time and RRA revenues exceeded $31 million, RRA was hit by a fire that very nearly destroyed the New York headquarters and left the firm badly shaken from the top down.

It was Mother's Day. The firm had just expanded its New York headquarters at 245 Park Avenue, installing our customary nice decor under the tasteful eye of Betty Sherrill of McMillan & Co. decorators. I was on my way to play tennis in Greenwich when I got a phone call from Ted Kister, RRA's chief financial officer, from New York. Kister said there was "a little smoke in the building." Where was it, I wanted to know. "Well, they aren't sure. They thought it might be near where we are."

"Well, you know, Ted," I replied, "we better get the facts. Like what the hell happened?"

Ten minutes later, Kister called back. "Actually, the fire was on our floor, and it was a lot worse than I realized. There was a lot of smoke." I threw on my business clothes, picked Kister up in Rye, and drove into New York that Sunday morning, reaching the office at noon. The first thing we noticed was that every window on our floor was open—not a good sign.

At least the elevator was working. But what we saw when we reached our offices is something I will never forget. Everything was the same color, smoke gray—the brand-new carpet, the desks, the drapes, the walls. It was like a black-and-white movie, with the contrast turned down. Firefighters were milling around, and an overwhelming acrid, sickening, burning smell hung over the whole office.

The fire began in our office services room, caused by faulty wiring in a new piece of equipment. The items that actually burned were relatively minor: personnel records and some equipment. But the white-hot heat generated a huge amount of smoke, which entered the air circulation system and was carried throughout the floor, covering everything with a foul-smelling gray blanket.

Initially, I tried to salvage some of it. A cleaning company came in three times to go over the floors, ceilings, and furniture with shampoo. But despite repeated scourings and fumigation, employees were still gagging on the smell. So the solution was to move the entire operation to another floor for nine months until we could move back in, even though the acrid smell never completely went away. I was able to rent vacant office space in the same building from Security Pacific Bank and move the entire group. The firm had installed a new computer in a separate room. Fortunately, it was fireproof.

The surprising thing is that despite the disaster, RRA continued to flourish. Morale was never better; business was never better; we were never better. In fact, it seemed that the crisis mobilized all of us and made us that much more committed to being successful. Today, as a souvenir of the fire, I have a grayish-green needlepoint pillow in my office imprinted with the words "Experience develops good judgment."

NOW FOR THE FUN PART

Never one to discount the value of motivational events— including parties—early on I established a habit of celebrating various milestones. Firmwide conferences dated from 1974, RRA's fifth anniversary, and were festive events at glamorous vacation destinations in the United States and abroad.

The first conference, at the Ponte Vedra Inn and Club in Ponte Vedra Beach, Florida, marked a milestone in that the group that attended, numbering over 100, finally convinced me that RRA had morphed into a growing, successful enterprise. I'd always had the mentality that you could go out of business at any moment and that you are only as good as your latest assignment. But at this conference, I remember walking into the room full of employees, and it suddenly occurred to me that we had a firm, and not just a few individuals scattered about. I had a feeling of tremendous corporate empowerment: we had really arrived, we were going someplace, and we could do anything we set our minds to.

We were also having fun. Tony Thompson, who was in charge of the conference, appeared at cocktails in a worker's uniform with a sign on his back saying "Russell Rentals," which was what people often mistook for the name of the business when they first heard it.

THE CIRCUS

Still, not every celebration was a resounding success. In 1979, RRA's tenth anniversary, I planned a big bash, this one at the Cloisters in Sea Island, Georgia. By this time, with spouses, invitees numbered about 200. So I decided to mount a special entertainment and hired the Florida State Circus, at a cost of $10,000, to entertain party guests.

On the day before the big event, the circus came to town and erected a huge tent, complete with trapezes and nets and seating for the crowd. The following day, the attendees were at a lecture titled "How to Be a Better Executive Recruiter" when RRA associate Steve Scroggins burst in, the blood drained from his face. "I've got to see you immediately," Scroggins said. "There's been an absolute disaster!"

"Oh my God," I said, thinking someone had probably been killed. Young Scroggins, who was about 30, was trembling and very nearly in tears.

"I don't know how to tell you this—it's so awful."

"What happened?"

"The tent blew down. The whole circus was destroyed. We have no entertainment, no program. We're dead. What are we going to do?"

I thought that no matter how bad it was, everything couldn't have been destroyed. So I asked Scroggins to find a local gymnasium, hire it, pick up the pieces, and set up what remained of the circus there.

He did just that, and the dilapidated performers managed to put on an event that was what I would euphemistically call a "partial success"—in other words, not a disaster.

EVOLUTION OF THE BOARD

As I gained confidence in myself and RRA's future, I kept thinking about strengthening our board of directors. Since it was an independent board, rather than an advisory board, I felt I had the great advantage of the members' unfettered business judgment, as well as an independent body to talk to regarding sensitive internal situations, including promotions, firings, and—most importantly—compensation.

The firm thus became that rare animal, a privately owned personal service company with an outside board. As RRA evolved, so did the role of the board. Looking back in his essay marking RRA's twenty-fifth anniversary, longtime board member John Beck says, "The board was not extraneous, but I don't think it played as important a role in the beginning as it does now. Today the board is very involved in the firm's activities. We consider ourselves a resource for the entire firm, really."

The board met twice a year, once in New York and once in an international location. Obie Clifford, who joined the board in 1984 to replace his father, recalls that as one of the original RRA investors, he was initially opposed to having an outside board. But he became a convert. "Pragmatically it has worked beautifully," he said later. "The board helped, particularly in the early days, to introduce clients. It gave the firm credibility; it provided a network the firm would not have had otherwise. And the board lent a certain panache to the institution."

Clifford also recalls fun-filled board meetings in Paris, San Francisco, Madrid, and Hong Kong. When George H. W. Bush was vice president and his brother Jonathan was on the board, the board was entertained beautifully in the Bush home, the official residence of the vice president on the Naval Observatory grounds. When Bush became president, Barbara hosted a reception for the wives at the White House.

Attracting suitably high-profile board members became a critical activity. Take, for example, my efforts to attract international investment executive John Loudon, Jr., son of the former chairman and CEO of Royal Dutch Shell petroleum. It was the early 1980s, and RRA had opened offices in London, Paris, and Madrid. I felt the board needed a distinguished international businessman to support its growing European operations.

Over lunch with Loudon in London, I communicated my desire to add a "deeply sophisticated" international businessman to the board, someone knowledgeable about the world of commerce but above having any commercial self-interest in being on the board.

Loudon was not receptive. However, a few weeks later, he called me and suggested that RRA consider his father, 70, who had retired from the oil giant founded by his family generations earlier.

The senior Loudon and I subsequently met in New York at the River Club, in its beautiful dining room overlooking the East River. I asked Loudon Sr. why he might be interested in joining the RRA board. Loudon frankly explained that because of his age he had to retire from the boards of IBM, Ford, and Chase Bank, though he was still serving on the Intel board.

I gingerly brought up the topic of RRA's board. Loudon pushed all the right buttons. Most importantly, he asked, "Do you want me to get business for you?"

"Of course not!" I replied. "We want friendship, good advice, and name recognition with a highly successful person like yourself."

After discussing fees, Loudon took the highly unusual move of offering himself as a board member without compensation, functioning simply as a friend and advisor. "Why don't we look each other over for a year and see how it goes?" he offered.

That was the beginning of a relationship that lasted for more than 15 years. When Loudon was 85, he tried to resign, but the offer was not accepted. We remained close friends until his death a few years later.

TRANSITION

As the firm neared the end of its second decade, the economy was recovering from the crash of October 1987, when the stock market had lost 22 percent of its value in a single day. Despite the shock to the economy, the market dive ultimately proved beneficial for RRA, as organizations pushed harder to find exceptional management talent. In fact, 1988 proved to be one of the most productive years in RRA's history.

With a weakened dollar, industrial companies saw increased demand for their products. Financial firms looked for new executives to help them reorganize and implement new strategies. More recruiting was done overseas, and international assignments at RRA reached nearly half of the total. RRA created an employee stock ownership plan, enabling 225 employees to participate directly in the firm's progress.

There were also important management transitions within RRA itself: While I remained CEO, I named Hobson Brown, Jr., who had joined the firm 11 years earlier from Morgan Guaranty Trust Co., president of RRA in 1987, replacing Ferd Nadherny. Lee Getz, my original partner when the firm was founded, decided to leave at the end of 1988, two years after the tragic and premature death of his wonderful wife, Connie.

When Hobson Brown became president of RRA in 1987, he wrote: "Our challenge is to be seen as the firm that provides the most consistently high-quality service on a worldwide basis, giving the same kind of service in Singapore as we do in London or Sydney or New York. That's why we have invested in technology. That's why we have strengthened our research capability. These things are designed to give us an advantage as a worldwide competitor without losing sight of the fact that there's always a local market in which we also have to be the best."

When I was a young banker at J.P. Morgan, we believed that the institution was more important than the individual. We also felt that a seamless transition in the evolution of senior management was a worthy objective. At this point in my life, I felt comfortable in moving on from RRA because I believed that the firm had gelled as an institution.

CHAPTER 7

THE BIRTH OF RSR PARTNERS

In 1993, I assumed the title of Founder & Chairman of Russell Reynolds Associates (RRA) with a contract to act as a consultant. I retained an office at the firm for a while, along with a mandate to help. But I felt that when the founder of a company retires, he should leave completely, clearing the way for the next generation. And so I did.

After briefly pondering a life of travel, fitness, sailing, skiing, fund-raising, politics, and civic involvement, which I had been doing all along anyway, I realized that retirement was not all it's cracked up to be. So RSR Partners, originally the Directorship Search Group, was formed in 1993, the same month I left RRA. The company initially focused on three businesses: board recruiting and consulting, the *Directorship* magazine, and director education.

In 2005, we decided to spin off the unprofitable publishing and director education businesses so that we could devote all our resources to what we did best: recruiting. The publishing and education businesses are now part of the National Association of Corporate Directors. As the executive search business was what I loved the most, I wanted to build a firm that would try to capture the great J.P. Morgan culture from the 1940s through the 1960s. Unfortunately, over the years, mergers and the information age have eroded what was great about the Morgan culture, including commitment, loyalty, and trust. I wanted to create a firm that embodied those values and that was relentless about the quality of our work, doing whatever was required to make our existing relationships stronger. Most service firms fail when they become compilations of individual performances rather than the power of collaborative group achievements. When trust, transparency, and authenticity are no longer a part of the culture of a service business, the soul of the firm begins to erode. But its clients are the ones who suffer the most. Using our board recruiting and consulting practice as the core of the firm, we decided to expand our industry and functional expertise primarily by attracting practice leaders from the search business who embodied our more nostalgic firm values. At my first firm, I made it a practice to identify promising professionals for our firm who began their careers outside the executive search business. I would then hire them and teach them the search business as we practiced it. RSR Partners, by contrast, has been built with people we have known and respected over the years.

Tom McLane, a Yale classmate and fellow Whiffenpoof, spent two decades working with me at RRA before joining RSR Partners in 1998. As a veteran of both my firms, McLane observes that RSR Partners operates on a different business model from that of RRA. Managing Director Carter Burgess was formerly a principal at Egon Zehnder, for instance, while Nona Footz was a client partner at Korn/Ferry's life sciences practice. Timothy O'Brien, originally trained at RRA, was a partner at Heidrick & Struggles, and Bruce Robertson was head of the North American CMO practice at Heidrick & Struggles.

My son, Trey Reynolds—like me, an alumnus of J.P. Morgan—also worked at RRA before becoming a managing director at RSR Partners, where he helps in every area of our business, including overseeing the firm's overall administration, technology, and finance, as well as the board, telecommunications, and technology practices.

More recent additions include Brad McLane (son of Tom McLane), a veteran of my former firm, who joined us in Chicago in 2011, and Wendy Murphy, a former Heidrick & Struggles human resources senior recruiter, who is Managing Director and head of the firm's Chief Human Resources Officers' Practice. Others include Managing Director Jason Ward, who heads up our global industrial practice, formerly a senior client partner at Korn/Ferry; Managing Director Mary Ellen Russell, formerly a client partner at Korn/Ferry; and Gary Matus, formerly a managing partner of Egon Zehnder International, who heads up the Los Angeles office. Colin Graham also recently joined us from Korn/Ferry. In 2012, we have added Charles Stonehill, a top-level British-born investment banker from Credit Suisse, Lazard, and Morgan Stanley, to run financial services, and Joe Bailey, former CEO of the Miami Dolphins, to head our sports practice.

After hiring some dynamic, seasoned recruiters along with some fabulous young people with great potential, RSR Partners has continued to build on its strengths. We now maintain offices in New York, Greenwich, Chicago, Cleveland, and Los Angeles.

BRAND POWER

Another hurdle was the ongoing problem of separating RSR Partners' new corporate, as well as my own personal, identity from that of my former firm RRA, which of course was and remains a major industry presence.

With my name still on the door of my former firm, it was just too easy to confuse the two companies. On many occasions after the founding of RSR Partners, friends or business acquaintances would approach me at a business function or cocktail party, greeting me with the words, "Russ, we just gave your firm two new assignments!" At that time, we were small enough that I knew it was not our firm to which these assignments had been awarded. But there was nothing to do but grin and bear it, so I'd smile and say, "They'll do a great job."

To further illustrate the brand name confusion, during the summer of 2009, I was in Chicago with RSR Partners' managing director and chief operating officer, Brett Stephens, making business calls. We planned to visit food industry giant Sara Lee and meet with then-CEO Brenda Barnes. We were going to ask whether Barnes was interested in joining a corporate board.

The morning of the meeting, we arrived almost late at Sara Lee and rushed in.

"Russell Reynolds here to see Brenda Barnes," I said to the receptionist. Then I saw another man waiting. He looked exactly like Matthew Wright from London, the CEO of RRA.

We greeted each other cordially.

"I'm here to see Brenda Barnes," I said.

"That's funny—so am I," Wright replied.

We soon realized that two meetings had been set up at the same time by mistake, one with me and one with Wright, the CEO of my eponymous firm.

"Matthew, you go to the meeting, and I will leave," I said.

"No—you go," he said.

"We are just here hustling business," I countered. "I'll go with you to the meeting and play the role of founder and chairman."

Again, Wright insisted, "No, you take the meeting, and I will leave."

I wound up taking the meeting, and it was the power of the name that made the difference. Wright got into a cab and went back to the airport, a true gentleman!

Once in the meeting, I said, "Brenda, you have a problem. We [RSR Partners, my new firm] are not doing work for you. Russell Reynolds Associates is. I think you should call Matthew Wright and apologize."

Barnes thought for a moment, realized that the whole thing was a misunderstanding, and had a good laugh. As it turned out, she had no interest in joining any corporate boards, which was the purpose of our calling on her. But the episode showed me just how hard it would be to separate the identity of RSR Partners from that of my former firm, a dilemma that is fortunately disappearing.

RSR PARTNERS TODAY

Today Brett Stephens, who joined RSR Partners in 1999, is the chief operations officer and managing director of the firm. Stephens has been taking on an increasing role in governance issues, board, and executive recruiting. "RSR Partners is now a significant player in the recruiting industry. The company has brought together a group of individuals who care about each other as much as they care about their clients," Stephens says. "We have opportunistically built the business by attracting leaders in different fields who have magnetic personalities, while ensuring that our core values and principles are never sacrificed for the financial rewards. You could say that the firm has grown to become a family. While everyone is unique, we all genuinely care about each other and do everything we can to support, encourage, and help our partners' activities and interests."

Managing Director Tom McLane specializes in board recruiting and corporate governance consulting. Recent searches included two for the Moscow School of Management Skolkovo, located outside of Moscow, through our affiliate RSR Russia, led by former RRA colleague Mike Tappan. The school needed non-Russian advisory board members, chiefly CEOs of companies with an interest in Russia, to increase transparency and boost investor confidence. "If they have an all-Russian board, no one will invest," McLane says. "Whatever regulations Russia has covering the way boards operate, enforcement of them is all but nonexistent." McLane and Tappan set to work identifying the ideal candidates: prominent American executives who have both a reputation for integrity and an understanding of Russian business practices.

"We recruited John Faraci, CEO of International Paper Company, the largest paper company in the world," says McLane. "It had a 50% interest in Ilim Pulp, the largest pulp and paper company in Russia. We also got Andrew Gould, CEO of the global engineering and construction company Schlumberger. Anecdotally, in the course of this search, I met the recently named head of the McKinsey office in Moscow, Yermolai Solzhenitsyn, son of Russian literary and political legend Alexander Solzhenitsyn. There is no doubt we are in an interesting business that leads to many meetings with fascinating 'heads'!"

There is also no doubt about the increasing importance and responsibilities of corporate board members in America, but also abroad in countries that don't have a history of transparency. Multinationals in countries like Russia can look to recruiters like ours to help them build their corporate model while polishing their international reputation.

Corporate board searches open doors all over the world, offer a look into the inner workings of major multinational companies, and can take unexpected and interesting turns, McLane recounts. "Shortly after I recruited Sir Peter Mason, CEO of the major construction company Amec Pic, to the board of Acergy (now Subsea 7), the CEO of Acergy surprised the board by saying he wanted to retire early. We were then engaged by this undersea engineering and construction company in the UK to recruit a successor CEO. The successful candidate was Jean Cahuzac, a Frenchman who was president of Transocean in Houston. During the course of the project, we were asked to assess six insiders, each of whom was a step away from being qualified for the CEO role. Cahuzac had been a resounding success and is now CEO of Subsea 7 following the merger of that company with Acergy, and Sir Peter Mason became lead director of the merged companies."

THE SEARCH PROCESS

Our firm uses a proven approach for completing comprehensive searches. Our objective is to identify, attract, and evaluate outstanding candidates from whom clients can select individuals who meet or exceed their organization's standards and who can help the company attain, even surpass, its goals.

In the first phase, position analysis, the recruiter meets with the client to understand not just the client's organization, working environment, specific requirements, and objectives, but the role the selected individual will play in the organization. The recruiter wants to get a sense for the type of candidate who will best fit the personality and culture of the organization.

The research phase begins with a careful analysis of relevant organizations, but the bulk of the search involves personal contact, following up leads within our own extensive database and our well-established network of personal contacts. Prospective candidates are extensively screened, with perhaps a dozen surviving the process. Each round of talks with candidates eliminates a percentage of the group by comparing and contrasting backgrounds and experiences. The recruiter then conducts intensive face-to-face interviews with the most promising candidates. He or she also considers the specific requirements: work experience and background, education, personality and managerial style, professional development, growth and achievement, and the ability to handle the position.

Résumé inflation is nothing new, but the Internet has changed the due diligence process dramatically. It has necessitated an even more thorough approach. Needless to say, all backgrounds and references are investigated thoroughly. Documentation includes references from prior managers verifying position functions and accomplishments, and performance strengths and weaknesses. These written references are accompanied by detailed reports on the selected candidates.

Communications with the client and the candidates during the search process are maintained in a way that respects both the confidentiality and sensitivity of the search agreement. RSR presents each prospect to the client for preliminary evaluation, arranges interviews and coordinates travel schedules, and follows up with candidates after each visit to determine their level of interest and to address any concerns.

When an offer is extended, RSR participates and assists in the discussions; and once the candidate starts the new position, RSR remains in contact with both the client and the candidate to ensure a smooth transition and a satisfactory completion of the assignment.

ADVISORY BOARD

Although a key activity of the firm is our board practice, RSR Partners itself operates with an advisory board rather than an outside board of directors. The members of the advisory board include such noted executives as Dana G. Mead, retired chairman of MIT and the former chairman and CEO of Tenneco, Inc.; James W. Kinnear, the former president and CEO of Texaco; Donald K. "Obie"

Clifford, president, Threshold Management, Inc., and former director of McKinsey & Co.; James B. Hurlock, retired managing partner of White and Case; L. Scott Frantz, our extremely capable Connecticut state senator and president of Haebler Capital; William F. Andrews, chairman of Corrections Corporation of America; Doni L. Fordyce, founding partner of Stone Key Capital; Patrick W. Gross, chairman, The Lovell Group; Richard L. Murphy, president, The Landis Group; Adam D. L. Quinton, adjunct associate professor at Columbia University School of International and Public Affairs; and Jonathan J. Bush, president, J. Bush & Co.

A key member of the board, Edward A. Kangas, served as global chairman and CEO of accounting firm Deloitte & Touche. Kangas currently serves on the boards of five public and three private companies. He has been so active in the field that he was named Director of the Year in 2007 by the National Association of Corporate Directors and was honored in its Corporate Directors' Hall of Fame.

Kangas believes that the qualities we brought to RRA are in evidence at RSR Partners: "Russ doesn't just do searches; he has lasting professional relationships with companies. When a CEO says, 'I have to remake my board,' Russ is an ideal guy to call. Russ will come up with names very fast, and they are very good, and there is never a problem closing them."

Kangas recalls the situation in 2003 at Tenet Healthcare, where he is nonexecutive chairman of the board. At the time, the hospital operator was the largest publicly traded healthcare group in the United States. It ran into issues with the federal government over Medicare payments.

To facilitate successful discussions with the Justice Department, the company decided it needed to rebuild the board and set the stage for a new chapter in Tenet's history. It was decided that 9 of the 11 members of Tenet's board should resign, which they did. Two years later when Tenet had successfully settled with the government, Kangas told me that Tenet needed a well-known, highly respected board member to show that the company had passed its crisis and was serious about becoming a quality, good-performing healthcare company.

"It's Jeb Bush!" I said. And Trevor Fetter, Tenet's CEO, and Ed talked with Jeb, and he joined the Tenet board. It was an important day for Tenet, which is doing fine today. Bush has been a great board member.

It's hardly surprising, given this kind of performance, that RSR Partners has made board searches into a specialty. RSR Partners has the expertise to build entirely new boards, appraise existing boards, create advisory boards, and advise on matters relating to corporate governance.

In fact, a March 2012 presentation lists over 70 well-known companies among our current or former board-search clients, including Capital One Financial, CIT Group, General Motors, PepsiCo, ExxonMobil, JP Morgan Chase, Stanley Black & Decker, Tenet Healthcare, United Technologies, U.S. Bancorp, and Whirlpool. Going forward, Stephens adds, he expects that board searches will comprise approximately one-third of the business, with executive searches occupying the balance. However, the growth of the firm will be driven mostly around the quality of work we do in executive search, as evidenced by recent searches conducted by Graham Michener.

"We conducted the Wells Fargo Head of Healthcare M&A search in less than two months," Michener explains, "by pulling Leerink Swann's head of healthcare M&A. The same hour (5 p.m. on a Tuesday) that we made this completion, and having just been retained by R.W. Baird & Co., one of the world's leading middle market investment banks, to conduct an MD, Healthcare Services Investment Banking search, our client at Baird decided to resign and join Leerink without the knowledge of what we had just done. In the end, Baird asked me to help retain this individual, but ultimately decided he was better going to Leerink because of the broken trust. More importantly, Baird decided to fire the other major search firm in favor of giving RSR Partners the other three healthcare searches they were going to launch simultaneously. Our one search turned into four searches overnight!"

RSR Partners is now positioned as a leading minimajor search firm, steadily expanding its clients and the number of top-flight recruiters who serve them. Although known for our expertise in corporate governance and the swift, discreet, and satisfying execution of board searches, RSR Partners conducts searches for top management positions across all industries. I see our firm hopefully as a "firm of the future"; we are composed of very experienced partners, and yet we're small enough to be flexible, nonbureaucratic, and swift in our executions. In 2011, we doubled in size.

It is not uncommon for newly arrived partners to have a significant ramp-up period before their client base offers work to them at their new firm. Often this is measured in many months. This has not been the case with our partners, who hit the ground running.

Shortly after recruiting Jason Ward to lead our Industrial Sector, we had the chance to compete for an assignment to find a CEO of a global publicly traded multibillion dollar transportation company based in Asia. We got the assignment despite competing against the major global search firms, each of which has an office and employees in China.

Jason Ward won the search and then executed it quickly and successfully by filling out his team with the best qualified search professionals in the region. Rather than relying on the "readily available" wearing the same corporate colors, Jason, as our lead recruiter in transportation and logistics, assembled a best-in-class team tailored to that assignment.

When I am sitting in our New York office, on the thirtieth floor of 280 Park Avenue, I feel I have come around full circle to my roots in the search business. The private club car on Metro North is long gone, but I still get a kick out of walking up Park Avenue, watching the business world go by and pondering the career history of each suited executive. Despite technological innovations and the transformation of communications and media, old-

fashioned methods, including face-to-face meetings and the sensitive assessments of a person's reputation, still, in the end, carry the day. I thrive on the wonderful spirit of the people at RSR Partners—and their dedication, intelligence, and sense of responsibility—and that has kept me on an upward trajectory of continuous inspiration.

CHAPTER 8

EXECUTIVE SEARCH TODAY

FRAGMENTATION AND REGROUPING

Since its modern inception in the 1960s, the executive search field has been dominated by five firms: Korn/Ferry International, Heidrick & Struggles, Spencer Stuart, Russell Reynolds Associates (RRA), and Egon Zehnder. Alongside these firms, a small number of midsize firms and many boutique firms have sprung up. In the past decade and a half, many of these smaller firms have combined into worldwide groups or networks sharing the same brand name.

This consolidation gained impetus during the ravages of the 2008 financial crisis and protracted downturn. While statistics on the industry are hard to come by due to fragmentation and the large number of privately held firms, the Association of Executive Search Consultants (AESC) estimates 2010 net annual revenues for the global executive search industry at $9.81 billion. That puts it over $1 billion below the all-time peak in prerecession 2008, when revenues hit $11 billion.

The recession caused fee income to decline by nearly 33 percent in 2009, as revenues plummeted to $7.43 billion. But there is some good news for this rapidly evolving profession: the industry grew by 32 percent in 2010, putting it into full recovery mode and setting the stage for another year of growth in 2011.

The recovery was impressive, given the magnitude of the decline. Still, according to Peter Felix, AESC president, "It is not so surprising given the strong underlying forces that were driving the worldwide shortage of executive talent in 2008, and their immediate resumption as soon as some form of economic recovery became clear."

The shortage of global talent, he added, has been exacerbated by demographic shifts in the West, as well as demand from emerging markets and new challenges facing top management.

To identify these challenges and take the industry's pulse, the AESC launched a study in 2010 that involved both a global survey of 200 search consultants and one-on-one interviews with leading consultants. In a report resulting from the study, the AESC identified the following trends and key areas of concern for the industry worldwide:

- The impact of social networking
- Pressure on pricing
- More aggressive and growing competition
- Specialization
- Globalization
- The need to offer advisory services to add value
- The increasing role of search metrics

SOCIAL NETWORKING

The advent of the Internet along with social networking sites like LinkedIn has many implications, one of which is the increased availability of information about candidates. Since the same social networking sites are accessible to human resource departments, line managers, and search firms, the ability of search firms to have unique access to the talent pool is shrinking in importance.

A 2010 survey by Jobvite, a Burlingame, California, company that specializes in recruiting via social networking technologies, found that social media are increasingly used by corporate recruiters to find new employees. More than 600 human resource professionals participated in the online survey that found:

- 73 percent of companies use social media to support their recruitment efforts.

- Among recruiters, LinkedIn is the most popular site, with 78 percent using the site to recruit, followed by Facebook at 55 percent and Twitter at 45 percent.
- 65 percent of companies have dedicated social media accounts with LinkedIn for recruiting. Another 39 percent have Facebook accounts for recruiting.

Says Jobvite, "The dramatic growth in the availability of online profiles and professional information on the web is changing the landscape of recruiting." This trend has put more emphasis on the other parts of the executive search model. Specifically, the added value of executive search has been more closely examined. In some cases, search services have been "unbundled," with only research, for example, requested by the client, allowing the client to perform the rest of the search.

Another change is that clients are more likely to assign only the most senior or complex searches to external firms, opting to perform the remainder in-house.

In this technology-enabled environment, the AESC reports that the personal connections of the recruiter relationships are becoming more important than ever: "Personal relationships will continue to drive performance, and a reputation for performing important work will continue to carry the day." The AESC goes on to say, "There will always be a market for creative and timely counsel thoughtfully rendered."

At the same time, search firms have little choice but to embrace technology. While a client can use Facebook and

LinkedIn for some search work, there are still other things that search firms can do that clients find valuable. In the AESC survey, clients commented on what they continue to value about executive search:

"Proven trustworthiness and integrity"
"The honest evaluation of candidates"
"The ability to present a wide range of good quality
    candidates"
"The assessment of talent"
"Knowledge of our industry and of candidates not
    previously known to us"
"Ability to surface a diverse slate of candidates"
"Search firm discipline and process"
"Expertise and insight into the marketplace, trends,
    best practices, competitive landscape and access to
    top talent"

For my own part, I believe that technology has made recruiting firms more valuable than ever. An executive search firm is working in your best interest and carefully sifting fact from fiction in LinkedIn profiles and Facebook pages. Recruiters do the necessary due diligence, and their reputation is on the line. But you are also paying them for their opinion, not just their work. A good company should know who its recruiting firm is. It can help in many ways beyond just procuring executives. A good friend is worth many acquaintances; what matters in life are relationships.

NEW PRICING PRESSURES

Partly as a result of an emphasis on cost controls, the fee structure of the search industry is coming under increasing pressure. Many clients are aggressively negotiating pricing by requesting reduced fees, fee caps, and detailed expense reporting. Some have required amended stage payments, especially in the financial services industry.

Henry Higdon, managing partner of Higdon Braddock Matthews LLC in New York City, observes that while in some cases the standard fee remains one-third of the first year's compensation, plus expenses, more clients are asking for a flat fee or a cap, particularly in the hedge fund industry, where annual compensation can run into hundreds of millions of dollars or more. "The trajectory has been clear," he states. "Now, there are caps on fees."

Other new clients, particularly private equity firms, are seeking more "skin in the game" and are asking that more risk be assumed by the search firm. "Sometimes the added value or complexity of the search process is not as apparent as those in the profession may wish to believe," the AESC opines in its report. The group adds that these cost pressures are generating considerable concern within the industry, as they bring into question the fundamental reason for charging on a retainer basis.

While these pressures are likely to fluctuate along with the market and economy, it is clear that the stability of pricing in executive search is under siege, a trend that will decrease margins unless productivity increases or the level of search assignments rises. Says the AESC, "The pressure on pricing is relentless, and can be expected to continue unless different business models are explored."

MORE AGGRESSIVE COMPETITION

In addition to the familiar competition from other search firms, the industry is increasingly facing a business threat from internal search firm professionals. The AESC survey clearly indicated a trend toward a larger percentage of search work being performed by internal search departments in large companies. Moreover, more organizations say they are thinking about creating such departments.

The AESC's conclusion: "Where a client organization has developed a well organized and effectively compensated internal search function, it may perform as much as 80 to 90 percent of available search work."

As competition intensifies for external searches, more recruiting companies report that they are participating in "shootouts" to secure mandates, as clients increasingly want them to prove that they have the specific skills and market knowledge to conduct the search in question, rather than relying on their general search expertise.

One way that search firms respond to this is via formal presentations to the prospective client, often including market mapping and organization profiles to secure a competitive bid. No matter how fast the internal search function grows, however, a small percentage of top-level work will always be reserved for the search industry, due to the complexity, visibility, and confidentiality of the jobs in question.

SPECIALIZATION

In the early years of executive search, the handful of leading firms dominating the industry, including my old firm, RRA, operated as generalists, conducting searches spanning a wide range of industries and functions. As the expansion of RRA illustrates, it was not considered desirable to concentrate too much talent into a single area—even one as lucrative as financial services. (For example, a key reason I hired Ferdinand Nadherny in Chicago was to expand the firm's expertise into the industrial heartland of the Midwest.)

However, over the course of the past two decades, the trend has been to specialize. The larger firms and global networks are now likely to organize themselves into cross-border teams to bring specialized knowledge to bear on a particular industry or function.

And in fact, when Hobson Brown took over as president of RRA in 1987, one of the first strategic moves he made was to accelerate the change from a geographic approach, in which there are many offices staffed with generalists, to a more focused approach, in which there are a smaller number of offices, each having an industry specialization. "A purely geographic approach tended to duplicate everything in every location," Brown wrote in an article commemorating RRA's twenty-fifth anniversary. "What we have done—particularly in the United States— is to take offices and make them 'competency' centers, so that there's a group of people within each office who covers a specific industry or maybe two industry groups. They become an institution, and when you have enough of them, they have a life beyond any one person."

Smaller firms and boutiques, such as my current firm, RSR Partners, now tend to select one or more specialties in which they can offer clients a track record and specific industry knowledge in order to compete successfully.

There are still generalist firms and consultants, particularly at the highest levels in smaller markets. But even among these firms, many are considering whether to become more specialized. In its survey, the AESC reported that among the 21 percent of respondents who described themselves as generalists, more than half said that within the next five years they will become, or are likely to become, more specialized.

GLOBALIZATION

While executive search has always been a global field, many firms are now expanding into newer areas like Eastern and Central Europe, the Middle East and North Africa, China, Russia, India, and Latin America. Accordingly, the balance of industry revenue globally can be expected to change during the next 10 years in favor of the developing world, although North America still remains the largest market for executive search, followed closely by Europe, Asia-Pacific, and Latin America.

ADVISORY SERVICES

One way to counter pricing and competitive pressures is for search firms to move beyond their core business and offer additional services—what the AESC calls "leadership services."

These consulting services include management audits, board and governance advising, executive coaching, succession planning, human capital strategy, and on-boarding.

At most firms, these services do not automatically come with executive search assignments, although they are sometimes prompted by them. In many cases, these consulting services have their own compensation models and fee structures, but a search firm may decide to integrate them into its overall servicing of a large or important client.

The majority of leadership advisory services, however, are sold as separate projects on an as-needed basis. And while they may be identified and sold by search firms, they are usually performed by colleagues who are experts in the field.

Interviews with search firms identify advantages as well as significant challenges in offering these services.

Among the advantages, the AESC found that added services broaden the discussion with clients, paving the way for a deeper, more lasting relationship. From a business standpoint, these services also provide an added source of revenue that may be countercyclical and in addition provide a competitive edge over and differentiation from other firms.

On the minus side, however, there is the issue of whether a firm possesses the skills and resources to compete effectively and build a reputation that will enhance, rather than detract from, its core business. While some search firms are well placed to offer these services, others are less capable. RSR Partners specializes in executive and board searches.

Importantly, the culture, operating methodology, and business dynamics of leadership advisory work are different from executive search work. Search work requires a task-oriented approach set on completing a short-term project, while leadership advisory services demand strategic, conceptual skills. Compensation models vary accordingly.

The perception of conflicts of interest also has to be considered. Confidentiality and data privacy can become an issue and may vary depending on the service offered. On the other hand, other professional service firms, notably accounting firms, have successfully diversified their offerings and have overcome potential conflicts of interest via full disclosure or the creation of Chinese walls in sensitive areas like data management.

My personal view is that firms that diversify their services will ultimately have the client conflict-of-interest problems that the management consulting firms noticed 50 years ago. The clients won't like it. Our view is that doing executive and board searches really well is a sufficient challenge for us at RSR Partners.

SEARCH METRICS

As concern over expenses increases, along with controls over the search function, it's not surprising that search metrics—measurements of the effectiveness of the search firm—are growing in importance. Widely used metrics include speed of candidate delivery, diversity, quality, satisfaction of the line manager, and long-term performance of the successful candidate.

Clients often favor speed of delivery, since it allows them to make rapid judgments about the effectiveness of the search firm in carrying out the assignment. This is one area where specialized boutique firms such as RSR Partners may have an advantage, since they can demonstrate that they know their market well, have done recent searches in the area, and are able to submit talent quickly to the client.

The more traditional approach of presenting a full short list in the same time period has largely gone by the board, especially in fast-moving sectors such as technology or financial services. The traditional approach is still favored, however, in assignments for nonprofit organizations or board searches, where a panel interview process may still be appropriate.

THE OMNIPRESENCE OF TECHNOLOGY

Back in the 1960s, we were entering information on cards through which holes were punched and rods were inserted. Files were housed in a contraption that went around on a belt and was so heavy that the floor had to be reinforced to hold it.

Needless to say, computers and technology have revolutionized that process. "The impact of technology is huge," says Russell S. "Trey" Reynolds III, my son and managing director of RSR Partners. Trey heads up the firm's technology and telecommunications practice and oversees its research and administrative activities.

Via the Internet, he says, "We can find out very quickly where the people are." The availability of so much instant information on the Internet, he adds, has prompted many companies to set up internal search departments and do more recruiting themselves.

The late Robert V. Lindsay, a good friend, former RRA director, and retired president of J.P. Morgan, personally witnessed the technology revolution and its impact on executive search. His view was that the impact has largely been positive. "The computer allows in-depth research and gives individual people access to the files much more efficiently and comprehensively," he says. "When you talk about computers and the business, those are two different subjects. The ability to have instant information is a tool—the computer makes managing the business more effective."

The one key thing that remains unchanged, he added, "is that this is an entrepreneurial business right down to the first person joining the firm."

I agree. While the computer and electronics have transformed the way files are kept and searches are done, some essentials have not changed. It's just a better filing system. Today's technology has no impact on the intuitive ability of a person to be a better recruiter. But it can make your life a little bit easier, and it certainly makes your assistant's life a lot easier.

From the client's point of view, the Internet has also made it easier for companies to do their own initial sourcing of candidates. Anybody can source using LinkedIn, Google, Spoke, ZoomInfo, Jigsaw, and other sites. On the candidate end, the Internet is also playing host to many job placement sites, including Monster.com and TheLadders.com, specifically targeting mid-to-high-level candidates.

INCORPORATING THE INTERNET

When candidates can discover and land C-level positions paying in the hundreds of thousands of dollars using such sites, some say the pressure is on for search firms to incorporate the Internet into their business more fully.

Peter Felix of the AESC says the best executive search firms and most skilled consultants are finding ways to adapt and thrive. The retainer model, for instance, is under some pressure, but it always has been.

Now, some search firms are offering more flexible fee arrangements. They are using the term *container* or the term *retingency* (both terms play on the words *contingency* and *retainer*) to show their willingness to use flexible recruitment models.

Another strategy is for firms to use the Internet to find and screen talent. For example, Korn/Ferry International recently created Futurestep (http://www.futurestep.com), formed in partnership with the *Wall Street Journal.* Futurestep is an Internet-based service targeted at providing companies with high-performing middle- to senior-level executives. It is designed to complete the recruitment process within 30 days, while providing total confidentiality and the highest level of service to both companies and applicants.

A new service, introduced by the AESC at its 2011 Americas Conference in New York City, is aimed at streamlining and adding value to Google searches. Called Vizibility, the service provides search firms with a SearchMe button or a link for Google that returns the correct results from Google along with the search string that was used to get them, saving time and heightening authenticity and relevance.

Clarke Murphy was a managing director and global leader of the CEO and board services practice at RRA in New York, and was recently elected president and CEO. Murphy worked for me for years at RRA, starting in 1989, and is an outstanding 22-year veteran of the industry. He is also a world-class transatlantic sailor. Murphy says that another impact of the growing role of computers is to push the industry to adapt to a shorter search process: "The mystique was the identification [of candidates]. Now it is the verification," he says. "Now, anybody can find people. A lot of that is publicly held information, and social networking makes it easier. It shortens the process, because identification [of candidates] is no longer the big issue."

While AESC's Peter Felix is confident that firms can adapt, Murphy is not as optimistic. "At the midsize level, the search business is probably going to go away," he predicts. "However, the most senior level work—C-suite level and direct reports—will not become automated. Verification of competencies and culture fit must still be done by personal assessment."

For executives looking to advance their career, these developments have indisputably made it easier to use the Internet to their advantage. They can familiarize themselves with electronic job sites and post their credentials where they feel comfortable. For better or worse, it is no longer necessary for them to rely strictly on developing a relationship with a recruiter to find that next job. Like today's savvy search firms, they can use technology to maximize results.

ETHICS ISSUES

At the AESC's March 2011 Americas Conference in New York, exhibitors included HireRight, Inc., an employee screening firm based in Irvine, California, that offers services for recruiters who choose to outsource part or all of the candidate screening process.

Much of this screening is Internet based, as the firm makes clear in its brochure. But as search firms increasingly parcel out screening work to service providers like HireRight, ethics issues arise. In a paper titled "The Ethics of Pre-employment Screening Through Use of the Internet," by Michael Jones, Adam Schuckman, and Kelly Watson, the authors argue that "as employers increasingly turn to the internet to research prospective employees, the ethical implications become . . . relevant and far-reaching."

Recent surveys report that over 25 percent of hiring managers consider Internet-based information when making hiring decisions. But the problem, as the paper points out, is that information found on the Internet is not always entirely factual. And even factual information on the Internet can be taken out of context, and so relying on it can lead to false conclusions. "It is unfair and unethical to base hiring decisions on false or irrelevant information," the paper concludes. Therefore, using the Internet to conduct pre-employment screening is possibly questionable.

Bill Radin is an industry consultant based in Cincinnati, Ohio. He points out that screening is a process that has many parts: "It includes whether the candidate meets the qualifications, is in a position to change jobs, reference checking, background checking, credit reporting, and so on. There are a lot of vendors. And there is also something called RPO, or Recruitment Process Outsourcing."

Recruitment Process Outsourcing is a new term describing the outsourcing of recruitment processes, mostly to India. It is a subset of business process outsourcing. In India, RPO is already a billion dollar–plus market and is expected to grow at a rate of 30 to 40 percent a year. The buzz phrase is enjoying a taste of success, with a number of corporate giants adopting the RPO model for their hiring needs, including British mobile Vodafone, Credit Suisse, HP, and Prudential.

On the ethical front, Radin points out that headhunting is not an industry in which there is regulation, licensing, or accreditation: "There is no equivalent to the National Board of Realtors or the SEC. Headhunting is basically a subset of sales. The only qualifications are a smooth voice on the phone and the ability to sound sincere. It is a self-congratulating and networking group."

It is also a secretive industry. There is no economic incentive to reveal anything, and since many firms are private, there is no obligation on the part of search firms to make financials public. "It is a very amorphous group of people," Radin says. "The big firms have their own marketing departments; there are thousands of boutiques. For every Korn/Ferry or Russell Reynolds, there are one hundred little guys."

In this freewheeling environment, he feels that technology—including Internet-based screening—has so far been a double-edged sword for executive search. "It is a Wild West of information out there. Now, anybody can know anything about anybody. But recruiters are needed to verify, screen and make judgments. I can [still] say that I add value. For example, does a person have value that may not appear in the data? Hiring is going to be a combination of DIY assisted through a third party."

Radin also points out that while technology has made information flow faster, information overload can also slow things down: "Technology has made the initial screening faster, but not the process. The process speeds up when the market is hot, and slows down when it is cool, regardless of the abundance of information. Technology can't produce a sense of urgency."

SALES AND RELATIONSHIPS

Recruiters can generate names and send résumés, but at that point the technology does nothing for me. It is still a sales and relationship business. Regardless of the ease of information distribution, the bottom line is that a company has to find and interview the individual. Ultimately, a hire cannot be made without an interview.

There will always be a personal relationship component. Recruiters will work their own network. Also, many searches must be done in confidence. Business is out there as long as there is a need to hire. Yes, information is readily available on the Internet. But, as they say, you get what you pay for. Companies hire people to solve problems, to create an asset, and to address needs. The intelligent recruiter will work from the problem to provide solutions, just like a good doctor.

GUT INSTINCT

Primitive or not, I believe that good recruiters now, as in earlier years, do not rely on the files. They rely on their instincts. They know who the people are, and when they go to a business meeting and get a new search, they have an idea of who the successful candidate is going to be, because it is all in their heads. Then they get on the phone and call people who they think would be ideal for the situation, based on their intuition and judgment.

And if a person isn't interested or can't be talked into it, he or she may recommend someone else—who is likely to be a carbon copy of the person.

People who spend a lot of time going through the files and doing research are frankly missing the boat. That's not what search is all about. Search is all about knowing people and understanding there is a bid and ask on everybody; the question is, what would it take to get them?

While the research department is a place where you keep the papers, a good recruiter knows who the candidates are in the field before he or she ever starts the search. You do your homework, you pick up the phone, you talk to a few people, and you walk in to see a top executive. But while you know who the players are, you don't tell the executive that. Often you get a more complete picture of the ideal candidate during the initial meetings. Then during the course of the conversation, when you're receiving the assignment, you dance around the subject and you dance around the specification, and the executive says, "Yes, yes, I like those people who smoke cigars," or "I like" something else.

What races people's motors is not just knowledge of the business; it's the fact that they have a common interest: they play bridge, or play golf, or collect antique cars, or attend the same church. Personal chemistry is a very important thing.

A DEEP BENCH

As a lifelong social networker, I tend to have my own inventory of candidates in my head. In fact, right at this moment, I can think of 50 people I could call in five minutes and get to come to my office on some opportunity or other, depending on what I said to them. Candidates also come from the recruiter's voracious reading of business publications such as the *Wall Street Journal, Forbes,* and *Institutional Investor.* Files get old fast.

As for résumés that come in over the transom, about 98 percent are thrown away, because those people are, generally speaking, not the best candidates. The art of the search business is to get stars, not just to fill a job. Stars are found through knowing people.

Still, only 1 out of 10 candidates is a real star. Today's technology, where we use the computer for so much, is different from the earlier system for recruiting. But in some ways it is the same, because it is still a filing system. It has almost no impact on the intuitive ability of a person to be a better recruiter, but it can make your life easier. And it can certainly make your assistant's life easier. But it still comes down to instinct.

FIGHTING BACK

For my own part, I feel that what is needed in the current environment is an offensive to improve the industry's image. On that score, I started the Executive Search Forum years ago with the CEO and number two person of the five major search firms. While the group met fairly often, its impact was limited.

The top search firms should be viewed by the clients as an indispensable source of good advice, wisdom, service beyond just doing a search, and execution. Now, there are many who see search as a commodity that is put out for bids on every assignment. So we need to fight back. Companies should know about the expertise and integrity of their search firms and respect the firms as the fine companies they are, just as they respect the accounting firms, banks, consulting firms, and law firms. We as an industry have not yet put ourselves quite on that level.

This could be done by tying in with a top business school or a professional organization. Regarding the low barrier to entry and the lack of qualification requirements, professional search executives should be accredited, much like attorneys or accountants. They should have training in human resources laws, tax laws, compensation, Sarbanes-Oxley, stock options, benefits, and more. The bar to entry should be raised, and that would be easy to do: there should be simple tests, certificates of compliance, and periodic checkups. People already in the business who are fearful could just be grandfathered in so they would not have to worry about it.

Getting the right people is the main reason that businesses are successful. Comparing ourselves with other search firms is fine, but we want to be compared with the best businesses in the world, not the best search firms.

The world has indeed changed from the clubby days when Gardner Heidrick, Spencer Stuart, Ward Howell, and I were the industry's Strategic Planning Committee. But for me, the simple idea of getting better people in order to do a better job has stayed the same—and will not be legislated out of popularity. Technology and its advances are important, but it would be a mistake to think the world has changed because of it.

A large part of the search business will remain an art and not a science. The process of getting top-quality, honest, dependable executives will always require good judgment, not just speedy identification with little discernment. The art of recruiting is to put two parties together who are like-minded and who have with the willingness to help other people more than themselves.

CHAPTER 9

MASTERING BEING RECRUITED

To the recruited, sometimes the methods of recruiters can seem all smoke and mirrors. But really it's quite straightforward: get the facts straight and present them professionally. A good search involves a deep understanding of the client company and its challenges, goals, and corporate culture; an objective penetration of the identity, effectiveness, and style of a candidate; and management of the recruitment process with a firm, polished, and professional hand.

If knowledge is power, then the more you know about this process, the more influence *you* will have in managing it as a candidate and coming out on top in your dealings with the executive recruiter.

155

WHAT IS—AND IS NOT—
EXECUTIVE SEARCH

As a candidate, it is essential to understand the difference between a retained search firm and other types of recruitment or placement services. According to the Association of Executive Search Consultants (AESC), the main professional association for retained executive search, there are four key distinctions:

1. Retained search firms work with client organizations to fill senior-level management or specialized professional positions. A retained search is not economically feasible for filling lower-level positions.

2. Retained search firms work with clients on an exclusive basis. This means that only one search firm—and no other firm or agency—is working to fill that position.

3. Retained firms are *retained by the client organization* to fill the position. This means that the client pays the search firm to mount the search and present the most qualified candidates. A large portion of the search fee is typically paid before the search begins.

4. A retained executive search firm plays a consultative role, working with clients to define positions, qualifications, and potential sources of talent. The consultant may also offer insights regarding compensation, to attract certain types of candidates.

There are clear advantages to the client in choosing a retained search. They include confidentiality, expertise, and professionalism. In the early days of the search industry, the business was negatively tarnished with a reputation for being "clubby." No more—the industry has clearly matured into a competitive profession, with the best firms proving themselves again and again to the most demanding clients.

Candidates also benefit by working with a respected retained firm. Besides access to a hidden job market (retained searches are rarely advertised), candidates can count on receiving advantageous positioning. Even if a candidate does not receive an offer, the recruitment provides experience and contacts.

That said, it is important in life to remember who pays the bills. Search firms work for the hiring organization. They do not find positions for candidates, nor do they counsel candidates on their career goals or management skills, although they have the ability to do so. The interest of the client company is of necessity foremost in their mind. In the long run, a retained search often costs no more than a contingency search (if all goes well).

THE PROCESS

Here are 10 standard steps you can expect the recruiter to follow when conducting a retained executive search:

1. *Conduct the initial client meeting.* The hiring client meets with the search firm to outline search requirements, timelines, and future organizational strategy and mission and to get an idea of corporate culture.

2. *Perform a deeper client analysis.* The search firm will then begin a more thorough analysis of the hiring company, identifying key opportunities for the new executive and defining a candidate profile that fits into the corporate culture and organizational structure. Often this stage includes meeting key executives at the hiring organization.

3. *Do a market analysis and create a candidate specification.* Following this process, the executive search firm will complete a deep analysis of the market and create a compelling executive job profile. Market analysis will outline the competitive environment and influence the type of executive the search firm will look for.

   This process often includes a team of highly skilled researchers and results in a document that will be a reference throughout the entire search process: the candidate specification. The candidate specification or job description will contain detailed information about the role, responsibilities, the hiring client, and key opportunities presented by the executive job and will outline career and educational requirements.

4. *Execute a search strategy.* This stage will include a deeper analysis of the market, outlining key compa-

nies the recruiter may wish to research for executive talent and documenting all avenues that will be exploited in order to gain access to the top candidates in the marketplace. The research tools that form part of the search strategy will often include their own database, BlueSteps (a database of senior executives for AESC members), previously conducted market analysis, alternative Internet sources such as social networks, and, of course, their own network and contacts.

5. *Engage in name generation and candidate identification.* Within the executive search industry, the process of creating an industrywide and functionwide map of talent and a long list of potential candidates is known as *name generation* or *talent mapping.* After they have a high number of potential executives listed (sometimes 100+), executive search consultants and researchers will begin qualifying the potential targets and identifying whether they are suitable candidates.

6. *Approach, qualify, and interview to create a short list.* A series of internal meetings will continue throughout the candidate identification process, and the number of potential candidates will be reduced to 10 at most. This short list is achieved through detailed interviews that discuss the specifics of the executive job and that explore the candidates' backgrounds, competencies, and interest in the role. Many firms apply their own specific methods of client qualification at this stage.

7. *Do basic reference checking and present the short list to the client.* Before any candidate is presented to the client, search firms will complete basic background checking to verify the candidate's qualifications and executive career background. Provided there are no problems (modifications if there are), the short list will be presented to the client.

8. *Narrow to three to five candidates and perform thorough reference checking.* Following meetings at the previous stage, the client will work with the search consultants to narrow the candidate short list to just three to five potential senior executives. At this stage, the search firm will begin thorough reference checks (often using specialist firms such as Kroll) and provide final thoughts on the strengths and weaknesses of each candidate.

9. *Assist with offer and negotiation.* After a series of interviews and consideration of external references, the client will select its preferred candidate, and the process of salary and offer negotiation will commence. Often the search consultant will act as a mediator in this process to ensure both parties' needs are being met.

10. *Support onboarding and integration.* The search firm will assist with the integration, called onboarding, of the successful candidate into the workplace. The degree of involvement varies depending on the wishes of the CEO or the human resources head and any agreements made earlier in the search process.

Although the search has been successfully completed, the search firm will continue to maintain close ties with the hiring client and senior executive to ensure long-term satisfaction for both parties. And as a concluding note to this section, retained search firms will never recruit executives from a client company for a defined time period, usually two years, without the full agreement of all parties involved.

WHAT A CANDIDATE SHOULD EXPECT

In the AESC's Candidate's Bill of Rights, the association says there are five basic things you should expect from a retained search firm:

- *Confidentiality.* As a candidate, you assume some risk should your current employer learn about the search. You therefore have a right to expect the highest degree of confidentiality from the search firm.
- *Full disclosure.* To make the right decision, you must be given all the information you need about the search firm, the client, and the position.
- *Professional treatment.* The consultant should answer your questions honestly, be organized and prepared, and respect the time you are investing.
- *Adequate process details.* The consultant should tell you about the time frame of the search, the steps that lie

ahead, and whom you will need to meet before a decision is made.

■ *No pressure.* Your decision should never be hurried,
and you should not be pressured to accept an offer.
The firm should, however, make you aware of dead-
lines and the implications of making or not making a
timely decision.

HOW TO WRITE AN EXECUTIVE RECRUITER-WORTHY RÉSUMÉ

At various stages in this hiring process, executive recruiters send reports to clients. Clients in turn circulate the
reports throughout the company. The résumé you write
is in effect the report you are writing for the executive
recruiter to send to the client or for the human resource
department to send to the CEO of the company that is
interviewing you.

As someone who has been on the receiving end of
résumés for decades, I know a good one when I see it.
Authentic résumés are a reflection of the inner workings
of a person. The ones that are created by outside consultants or outplacement firms are instantaneously identifi-
able as hyperinflated versions of a whimsical career that
did not necessarily work out. You do not want to be in that
category. Here are some basic steps to follow:

■ Never delegate this responsibility to someone else. It is the most important first step in the hiring process, and you have the best chance of getting the job in question when you write your own.

■ Start your résumé with your name, address, e-mail address, phone number, cell phone number, and other ways to reach you. It is amazing how many people, especially senior people, send out bios without any way of reaching them, because the bios have been prepared for public relations purposes and not for identification purposes. We are living in a world of heightened anonymity and invisibility. Many companies do not even indicate where they are located on their websites; many people fail to identify themselves within an area because they use a cell phone number and an e-mail address. The entire résumé should say who you are, where you are, what you are, how you are (your health), and why you are. Mention your marital status if appropriate. If there are strong distinctions or extracurricular activities, such as sports or book publishing, list them.

■ Below your personal identification information at the top, list your inverse employment history, starting with the most recent and ending with the earliest. For each company you have been associated with, put down a sentence or two describing the firm, no matter how famous it is. In other words, say "Citigroup has assets of $1 trillion, employs 300,000 employees globally, and lost or made $XX last year." You want to make it easy for recruiters.

- With smaller companies, it is even more important to identify and describe the company. In those cases, you want to mention the management setup and explain where you fit into that structure. Attaching an organizational chart is not a bad idea.

- Prepare an additional page summarizing your compensation going back to your first job. Put in exact amounts—including all allowances, cars, stock option grants, 401(k) contributions, profit sharing, club reimbursements—to make the whole package as complete as possible. This page should be separated from the résumé and is used when a prospective employer asks for the information. The page shows you have been on the ascendancy and are successful, even if you are currently replanting yourself.

- Do not offer references with your résumé. That is defensive. It goes without saying that everyone has at least a few friends who will say something nice about them. However, when asked, think of a couple of people who may not necessarily be your best friends. Your credibility goes up as your honesty goes up. Everyone has a balanced story, and no one is perfect. The employer wants a balanced picture, and he or she ultimately becomes the judge, especially of people who have been terminated. Many of the most successful people in business—especially in the current economy—

have at one point or another been fired from previous jobs, or at least have departed as a "mutual decision."

You are the master of what you don't say and the slave of what you do. Always tell the truth, get the facts straight, and lace your résumé with supporting material, including annual reports and proxies. Sometimes a photo helps. Do not leave gaps in your work experience.

Also remember that it doesn't hurt if you think like a recruiter when writing your résumé. Recruiters review numerous résumés. Faced with competition of that magnitude, it's easy to see why your résumé has to be outstanding for it to get attention. Most people reviewing your résumé don't have more than a minute to decide whether they want to read it in depth.

Given the volume of résumés that recruiters review for each position, it's important to write your résumé in simple terms that someone who doesn't have a specialized background can grasp. As you develop the highlights from each of your previous positions, ask yourself if a stranger would understand what you've written.

List only significant work-related accomplishments, but include personal distinctions as well. Keep in mind, though, that because the average professional holds more than five jobs during his or her career, chances are good that some of your work-related accomplishments may not be relevant to the job you're currently being considered for. Don't overwhelm reviewers with information that they don't need.

165

NETWORKING YOUR RÉSUMÉ

Make up a list of the 20 businesspeople whom you have met and whom you admire most. These are the people you respect and who probably tend to admire you. Write them a letter on your personal home stationery (hard copy, not an e-mail), and attach your résumé, which is the prospectus of the greatest person in the world—namely, you. Avoid adjectives and hyperbole, and stick to the facts. Embellishing adjectives diminish the effectiveness of your presentation. The facts speak for themselves.

TIPS FOR DEALING WITH HEADHUNTERS

As the search progresses, here are some thoughts on dealing with the headhunter who has contacted you.

1. *Don't be afraid to negotiate.* A good candidate is necessarily a good businessperson, and a good businessperson is a good negotiator. A strong, astute candidate can sometimes cut his or her own deal. It helps to know your worth, have a suitably high opinion of yourself, and use chutzpah!

A number of years ago, Kennecott Copper asked RRA to find a new CEO. This was a company with billions in sales. I knew one of the top geologists at Exxon and went to ask his opinion of some of the candidates RRA had in mind for Kennecott.

He expressed an interest in the job himself, a big surprise to me. I told him it paid well and carried stock options on 25,000 shares. "You mean 250,000 shares," he said, as if correcting me. I told him that I thought that was a stretch but that I would try the figure out on Kennecott. He ended up making his own deal with the company and getting his 250,000 shares. He tacked his own zeros onto the stock option number, and Kennecott bought it!

2. *Do your homework.* A first-rate candidate will do research on his or her own—and sometimes can put the headhunter to shame. Take the case of John Byrne, an insurance executive who ended up running GEICO and Fireman's Fund. Before that, he was seriously considering becoming the CEO of another insurance company in New England.

He called me up one day and said, "I'm not so sure about that company."

"Why not?"

"Because on Sunday I spent three hours sitting in my car in the parking lot. All these people were going in and out of the accounting department. I think they have a problem."

He was right. Meanwhile, I got a call from a New York attorney with an urgent assignment from insurance giant GEICO: find a CEO before the company went bankrupt. "We don't have time to talk about the fee," he added.

I thought I was being outmaneuvered. I insisted, "Our fee is payable 30, 60, and 90 days after the assignment."

"Are you kidding?" he replied. "We have about eight hours!"

Lee Getz called John Byrne and asked if he was interested. "Absolutely," he said.

Within hours, Byrne had absorbed a great deal of information and decided that GEICO was manageable. He saved the company and made millions for its shareholders and himself!

3. *Practice the art of getting anyone to call you back promptly.* It's amazing how easy it is to contact people when you have something important to say. When Alexander Haig commanded NATO, before he became secretary of state, I decided he would be a good candidate for a search. I asked my secretary to call Haig up, but she didn't know how to reach him. "Call the Pentagon," I said, "and ask for Haig and see what happens."

Nothing useful happened. Then she called NATO in Brussels. Someone answered and asked what I wanted to talk to Haig about.

"Tell them," I said, "to tell the general that we have an assignment to recruit a CEO. It is an attractive offer that could make him a rich man. In view of his impending retirement, we thought he might be interested."

Twenty minutes later, the phone rang. A colonel said that the supreme commander of NATO was on the line. We had a friendly talk, and I asked Haig, "If it isn't a breach of international secrecy, where are you?"

"In West Germany," he said. "In a tank."

4. *Trust your own instincts.* When I was asked by *Chief Executive* magazine what advice I would give to a senior executive who aspires to become a CEO, I gave this reply: Be a professional. Don't fail to sell yourself, and make yourself known in the company. It's important to have some guile. In terms of long-term strategy, make sure you serve in several key managerial positions in the company and use them as stepping-stones.

Today's realities dictate that you should spend no more than three to four years in each position. In most places, if you get stuck in one job too long, your chances of moving ahead are dead. It goes without saying that one must be loyal to management and support the organization, which does not mean that one must submerge one's individuality into the group. But surely an essential skill of a leader is that he or she must know how to follow.

THE 20 QUESTIONS MOST OFTEN ASKED BY HEADHUNTERS AND HOW TO RESPOND

No two situations are ever exactly the same, but as a general guide, these are the types of questions that could come up in a typical interview.

1. WHY DON'T YOU TELL ME ABOUT YOURSELF?

This question, often the interview opener, has a crucial objective: to see how you handle yourself in unstructured situations. The recruiter wants to see how articulate you are, how confident you are, and generally what type of impression you would make on the people with whom you come into contact on the job. The recruiter also wants to learn about the trajectory of your career and to get a sense of what you think is important and what has caused you to perform well.

Most candidates find this question a difficult one to answer. However, the upside is that this question offers an opportunity to describe yourself positively and focus the interview on your strengths. Be prepared to deal with it. These days, it's unavoidable. Some recruiters may open with it as an icebreaker, and some may use it because they're still getting organized, but they all use it to get a sense of who you are.

There are many ways to respond to this question correctly and just one wrong way: by asking, "What do you want to know?" You need to develop a good answer to this question, practice it, and be able to deliver it with poise and confidence.

The right response is twofold: focus on what interests the interviewer, and highlight your most important accomplishments.

Focus on What Interests the Interviewer

Do not dwell on your personal history—that is not why you are there. Start with your most recent employment and explain why you are well qualified for the position. The key to all successful interviewing is to match your qualifications to what the interviewer is looking for. You want to be selling what the buyer is buying.

Highlight Important Accomplishments

Have a story ready that illustrates your best professional qualities. For example, if you tell an interviewer that people describe you as creative, provide a brief story that shows how you have been creative in achieving your goals. Stories are powerful and are what people remember most. A good interviewee will memorize a 60-second commercial that clearly demonstrates why he or she is the best person for the job.

2. How long have you been with your current (or former) employer?

This is a hot-button question if your résumé reflects considerable job-hopping. Excellent performers tend to stay in their jobs at least three to five years. They implement course corrections, bring in new resources, and, in general, learn how to survive—that's why they are valued by prospective employers. Your time in service is a vital part of your appeal to a future employer regardless of the good reasons you lack that golden credential.

If your résumé reflects jobs with companies that were acquired, moved, closed, or downsized, it is still viewed as a job-hopper's history. In this case, make an extra effort to know prospective hiring authorities—including recruiters—outside the hiring venue. Volunteer, and go to events where they may be found. Ratchet up your networking to include the country club—anything that exposes you to hiring authorities who can get past your tenure issue because now they know you. Your networking efforts have never been so important.

3. What is your greatest weakness?

An impressive and confident response shows that the candidate has prepared for the question, has done serious self-reflection, and can admit responsibility and accept constructive criticism. Sincerely give an honest answer (but not a long one), be confident in the fact that this weakness does not make you any less of a great candidate, and show that you are working on this weakness and tell the recruiter how.

4. We're considering two other candidates for this position. Why should we hire you rather than someone else?

Do not be distracted by the mention of other candidates. Focus on what strengths you bring to the table. These should be consistent with the things most employers are looking for in candidates during the job interview: competence, professionalism, enthusiasm, and likability. Remember, they are looking for chemistry between you and the hiring firm. Be prepared to summarize in 60 seconds why you are the best candidate for the job. Also, let the recruiter know you want the job and you will enjoy working with the hiring firm. A lack of interest in the job may indicate a lack of enthusiasm for the job.

5. TELL ME ABOUT A SITUATION WHERE YOU DID NOT GET ALONG WITH A SUPERIOR.

The wrong answer to this hot-button question is, "I've been very fortunate and have never worked for someone I didn't get along with."

Everyone has had situations where he or she disagreed with a boss, and saying that you haven't forces the recruiter to question your integrity. Also, it can send out a signal that the candidate is not seasoned enough or hasn't been in situations that require him or her to develop a tough skin or deal with confrontation.

It's natural for people to have differing opinions. When this has occurred in the past, you could explain that you presented your reasons and openly listened to other opinions as well. For example, "Recently, the CEO recommended a change to a report that in my opinion made the reporting more cumbersome and time consuming. I expressed my concerns but also asked questions to determine what information the CEO needed to capture that was not currently in the report. Once I understood his needs, I was able to offer a suggestion that satisfied the firm's information needs and actually streamlined the existing report, making it easier to use."

6. DESCRIBE A SITUATION WHERE YOU WERE PART OF A FAILED PROJECT.

If you can't discuss a failure or mistake, the recruiter might conclude that you don't possess the depth of experience necessary to do the job. The recruiter is not looking for perfection. He or she is trying better to understand your level of responsibility, your decision-making process, and your ability to recover from a mistake, as well as what you learned from the experience and if you can take responsibility for your mistakes.

Respond that you'd like to think that you have learned something valuable from every mistake you have made. Then have a brief story ready with a specific illustration. It should conclude on a positive note, with a concrete statement about what you learned and how it benefited the company.

7. WHAT LEVEL OF COMPENSATION ARE YOU EXPECTING?

As a screening device, recruiters often ask early in the interview what compensation you are looking for. Answer the question, fully prepared with all the facts, including base salary, cash bonus, stock awards or options, 401(k)

174

plan payments, healthcare, and other perks, including use of the company plane, and the like.

After providing all the compensation history, try to redirect salary questions with a response like this: "I applied for this position because I am very interested in the job and your company, and I know I can make an immediate impact once on the job, but I'd like to table future salary discussions until we are both sure I'm right for the job." If you ask for more than the employer is willing to pay (or occasionally, on the flip side, undervalue yourself), the recruiter can eliminate you before spending more time with you.

8. WHAT ARE YOUR STRENGTHS?

Describe two or three skills you have that are relevant to the job. Avoid clichés or generalities; offer specific evidence. Describe new ways these skills could be put to use in the position you are being considered for.

9. HOW DO YOU EXPLAIN YOUR JOB SUCCESS?

Be candid without sounding arrogant. Mention observations other people have made about your work strengths or talents.

10. WHY WOULD YOU BE INTERESTED IN THIS POSITION?

The most important qualities that a candidate can bring to a position are honesty and integrity. Be frank—if, for example, you are 41 years old and your boss is 42 and not likely to be replaced anytime soon, explain why you feel your opportunities may be limited. Often, after reviewing a candidate's situation, my advice is to stay put and not to make a job change. People often foul up their careers by making shortsighted moves.

11. WHAT DO YOU DO WHEN YOU ARE NOT WORKING?

The more senior the position, the more important it is to know about the candidate's qualities that will impact his or her leadership style: is the person well adjusted and happy, or is he or she a company zealot? Recent developments at Hewlett-Packard illustrate this point. HP's board was not fully briefed on some of the CEO candidates they hired.

Discuss hobbies or pursuits that interest you, such as sports, clubs, cultural activities, and favorite things to read. Avoid dwelling on any political or religious activities that may create conflict with those of the interviewer.

12. WHAT DID YOUR PARENTS DO? ARE YOU TAKING ADVANTAGE OF OPPORTUNITIES?

I ask this question because I feel it is indicative of motivation. If you are one of six children and your father is a police officer, you clearly had to work hard to get where you are. If, on the other hand, your father is a hedge fund manager who may make billions of dollars a year, your motivation may not center so much on financial gain. A brief, honest answer is sufficient.

13. WHY DID YOU LEAVE YOUR LAST POSITION?

At high levels, issues that relate to personality and temperament become more important than they might otherwise. The recruiter wants to know if you will fit in with the client company. The recruiter may also be fishing for signs of conflict that indicate a potential personality problem.

Be honest and straightforward, but do not dwell on any conflict that may have occurred. Highlight positive developments that resulted from your departure, whether it was that you accepted a more challenging position or learned an important lesson that helped you to be happier in your next job.

14. WHY DO YOU WANT TO WORK IN THIS INDUSTRY?

Think of a story to tell about how you first became interested in this type of work. Point out any similarities between the job you're interviewing for and your current job. Provide proof that you aren't simply shopping in this interview. Make your passion for your work a theme that you allude to continually throughout the interview.

15. HOW DO YOU STAY CURRENT?

Demonstrate natural interest in the industry or career field by describing publications or trade associations that are compatible with your goal. I am personally impressed by people who still read newspapers and watch business news channels closely.

16. WHERE DO YOU WANT TO BE IN FIVE YEARS?

Don't give specific time frames or job titles. Talk about what you enjoy, what skills are natural to you, what realistic problems or opportunities you'd expect in your chosen field or industry, and what you hope to learn from those experiences. You shouldn't discuss your goals in a field or industry unrelated to the job you're applying for. This may sound obvious, but too many candidates make this mistake, unwittingly demonstrating a real lack of interest in their current field or industry.

17. TELL ME SOMETHING ABOUT YOURSELF THAT IS NOT ON YOUR RÉSUMÉ.

Think of a talent or skill that didn't quite fit into your employment history but that's unique and reveals something intriguing about your personality or past experience. *Example:* "I've managed my own small portfolio since I was 16, and I've averaged a 12 percent return over the past eight years." If you are charitable, describe it.

18. TELL ME WHAT YOU KNOW ABOUT OUR CLIENT COMPANY.

Describe your first encounter or a recent encounter with the company or its products and services. What would be particularly motivating to you about working there as opposed to working the same type of job in a different company? The recruiter will look for evidence of genuine interest and more than just surface research on the company. Reciting the annual report isn't likely to impress most recruiters, but feedback from customers and employees will.

19. DO YOU BELIEVE YOU'RE OVERQUALIFIED FOR THIS POSITION?

Most people don't expect to be asked if they have a great deal of experience. This question could quite easily catch a candidate off guard, which is exactly the interviewer's intention.

Don't hesitate to answer this question by showing complete confidence in your ability. For example, "My experience and qualifications make me do my job better. My business experience helps me run the art department in a cost-efficient manner, saving the company money. My qualifications are better for your client too, since the client will be getting a better return on its investment."

20. WHAT WOULD YOU DO IF ONE OF OUR CLIENT'S COMPETITORS OFFERED YOU A POSITION?

The recruiter is trying to determine whether the candidate is truly interested in the industry and company or whether he or she has chosen the company randomly.

Contrast your perceptions of the company with your perceptions of its competitors, and talk about the company's products or services that you've encountered. In the long run, which players do you believe are most viable and why? This is also a good time to ask the recruiter for his or her opinion about why the client company stands out.

THE SMARTEST QUESTIONS TO ASK A RECRUITER

It is not enough simply to anticipate the questions you will be asked in the interview. It is also important to proactively ask questions of the recruiter that show you know the industry and the client company well and that you are in a position to carefully consider all aspects of any possible offer.

Usually, either before or after posing questions like the ones above, the recruiter will tell you the name of the company and the position's title, location, reporting relationships, responsibilities, and perhaps compensation. If the recruiter doesn't, don't be offended.

If the recruiter fails to tell you the name of the company, you will want to know why. The search, or details about the position, may be confidential. Or he or she may simply be holding back until you need to know or until he or she knows it has aroused your interest.

Here are key questions you should consider asking the recruiter:

 Why is the client looking for someone to fill this position?

- What happened to the incumbent?
- To whom will I be reporting?
- What are the company's plans for the future?
- Who is the main competition?
- What are future opportunities?

In the event that you are not interested, say so right away. There is no point wasting the recruiter's time, or yours. However, by way of building a continuing relationship, you should provide any leads to sources or other candidates that you can.

CHAPTER 10

EQUILIBRIUM

The most successful people I have known have balance in their lives. They have achieved an equilibrium that allows them to have a satisfying work life in the context of good health, a solid family life, good friends, and financial stability.

I see a recruiting assignment as a request for business equilibrium as well as a talent search. What is business equilibrium? It is the basic components of leadership that don't change over time—a set of values that we need to keep in mind as corporate recruiters with a vested interest in seeking out the best business leaders we can find. I view certain qualities as essential to achieving business equilibrium:

 Character. In essence, this is the ability to distinguish right from wrong.

 Feet on the ground. This is an instantly obvious characteristic that instills confidence. It implies an ability to hear what people are saying, not just what they want you to hear—a crucial distinction.

- *Good values.* Whether religious, ethical, or ideally both, these signposts are visible in any transaction. The challenge that people face in every business, regardless of what kind of business, is not whether to act ethically but how to make sure that they and their colleagues do act ethically. That gets to the issue of who sets standards for ethical conduct in an organization, how they are set, and who measures compliance with them. That's the leader's role.

- *Direction.* This refers to meeting expectations at every stage in a person's career. A friend who went from Harvard to New York University Medical School chose to intern at Bellevue. Why? Because the most brutalized people are there, and he could help as well as learn. Interns and residents who choose to go to Bellevue choose to be challenged, because Bellevue gets the most serious cases in its emergency rooms. There the aspiring medical professional will work the hardest and therefore learn the most. My friend is now a renowned pediatrician who was the head of his hospital for many years. I would have hired him many years ago, and I still would.

- *Consideration for others.* In business, as in other areas of life, this is a given, and yet it is all too rare in the executive suite.

- *Ambition.* Ambition was once limited for most CEOs to the company they worked for all their lives. In the

1960s, only about 7 percent of new CEOs had been with the companies they headed for less than four years. That number more than tripled by the early 1980s. It is still going up. Today these successful and ambitious "outsiders" include the heads of Hewlett-Packard, Browning-Ferris, Wang Laboratories, and Goodyear, to name only a few.

- *Dedication.* This derives from rising to meet a challenge, making the most of every opportunity, and leading a well-rounded life.

- *Good reflexes.* Effective leaders do things now rather than later. Many years ago, when Johnson & Johnson faced the Tylenol poisoning disaster, the company immediately removed the product from the shelves and came forward with the details along with advice for customers. Union Carbide immediately accepted responsibility for the Bhopal disaster in India, and the CEO flew there personally to take the heat—a sign of real leadership. Simply reacting, or seizing on excuses, is a mistake. I always think, "What you do next is very important," and look for this in candidates, too. I ask myself, "If her partner jumps out of a window on the fiftieth floor, will she follow him like a lemming, or will she take the elevator down and consider a better option?"

- *Education.* This is an essential. We live in a meritocracy, but it's difficult to show your merit if you haven't pursued the best education possible under your circumstances and then made the most of it. Education

185

is also tied to ethics. The basic values once put forward in American education are making a comeback after the excesses—financial and otherwise—of the economic crisis we are still living through.

- *Self-confidence.* No real leaders are averse to performing tasks that are supposedly beneath them. Self-confidence is a lot more than role playing and should not be confused with it. Self-confident business leaders don't actively solicit business, but they remain visible. In building a firm, the essence of executive recruiting is *noticing* who the best people are and then asking them to join you, confident that they will be as pleased with you as you are with them.

- *Humility.* Some of the most impressive leaders I know answer their own phones. When I called the late Walter Wriston's number at Citicorp for the first time and asked, "Is that you, Walter?" he replied, "Who did you expect?" That one expression of surprise said a great deal about him and his organization.

- *Self-knowledge.* People cannot be truly good at what they do without self-knowledge. One day a 20-year-old Cadillac pulled up in front of our house. An old man in a threadbare jacket got out and asked if we wanted to buy orchids. He said, "You are probably going to try to get rid of me or feel sorry for me, but actually I am a very good flower man. I can deliver flowers that are much better than you can buy in the stores, for less money, and bring them to your door. Now are you interested in talking to me?" "Absolutely," I said.

It turned out that he had gone to Harvard Business School and had given up being a stockbroker to sell flowers—which he knew he could do very well. He arrived at Christmas with two cars full of flowers, and proved to be a delightful person comfortable in his role, productive and with a sense of humor. He was a success, in my book, and a giver rather than a taker.

HANDICAPS

The largely self-generated problems of business leaders often go unnoticed until an executive recruiter is brought in to help rectify things. These problems are often so obvious that you would think anyone could instantly identify them, and yet in many cases the leader is the last one to do so.

Armand Hammer, the U.S. industrialist and long-time head of Occidental Petroleum, also had a reputation among some as a benevolent philanthropist. My introduction to Hammer grew out of a charitable effort I helped to organize in the United States to raise the *Mary Rose*, a Tudor ship that, in a dramatic turn of events, sank, fully loaded, just off Portsmouth Harbor after sailing off in battle in 1545. In this effort, I worked with Charles, the Prince of Wales and president of the British Court of the *Mary Rose*.

Along with a group of friends, I raised about $500,000, most of it donated to the English fund and the rest to Mystic Seaport and South Street Seaport. I had received a call from Prince Charles, asking me to go and see Armand Hammer to ask him for a contribution. His Royal Highness explained that in his position he could not make that solicitation, and so I agreed.

I spent the better part of an hour with Hammer, who spoke at length about his charitable endeavors curing cancer and working toward world peace. He finally said he would donate $100,000 if I could raise another $900,000, which we eventually did.

Later, Hammer suggested through intermediaries that the *Mary Rose* organization should be combined with his United World College, an effort to promote world peace, at the annual fund-raising event called the Broadlands Ball, held at the spectacular Mountbatten estate that is the home of Lord Romsey, Lord Mountbatten's grandson and a close friend of the Prince of Wales.

I thought that combining the two unrelated charities was not such a good idea, and I told Hammer as much. Apparently this did not go down well with him. The next thing I knew, I was approached at the Broadlands event by an English member of the *Mary Rose* organization, who politely suggested that I resign and find someone else to head the fund-raising effort in the United States.

This hit me hard. I had thrown myself into the project, entranced by the romance of raising the Tudor ship—with its load of cannons, armor, implements, and other priceless historic artifacts—off the ocean floor. And in fact, we had raised quite a bit of money. Pressing his point, he talked about the need for new blood. Having little choice but to agree—it was their show, after all—I asked if they had anyone in mind to replace me. "No one," he said. "You'll be the first to know."

A few months later I was on vacation in Maine. There was a thick fog; a fire roared in the fireplace, clam chowder was bubbling in the kitchen, and the soaring refrain of a symphony by Tchaikovsky provided the background music. Into this idyll our cook intruded and said, "There's a gentleman from England on the phone. He wants to talk to you about the *Mary Rose*." It was the man from the Broadlands Ball, who said, "I've got wonderful news! We have a new president for the organization."

"Oh really? Who's that?"

"Dr. Hammer."

Long after my astonishment had died down, I introduced Hammer at a black tie dinner at the Smithsonian in Washington. I said with sincerity that I had never met anyone who had greater input into the activities with which he was associated. Sad to say, very little was done in the United States for the *Mary Rose* after that.

That experience taught me that while it's good—even essential—to get involved in outside groups, and particularly charitable ones, it's equally essential to do so for the right reasons. Fortunately, in many instances, heads of groups like the *Mary Rose*, or senior wardens of a church, or heads of a hospital, are there as givers, and not takers.

Their motivation is altruistic. If it's an extension of your ego, let someone else do it.

GIVERS VERSUS TAKERS

People who grow into really great leaders are usually givers as opposed to takers. Their basic orientation is to help people become successful—to take an interest in what others want and to help them discover what they are truly capable of achieving.

Once at a conference on Long Island, I decided to sail my boat, a Sparkman and Stephens–designed 47-foot wooden yawl, back to Connecticut. I said that anyone who wanted to help me was welcome. The weather was beautiful but changed rapidly, and a hurricane cropped up in the forecast. By departure time, I had a crew of only two.

Both executives were associates in the firm, and either one could have been CEO of Russell Reynolds Associates (RRA). The sun was beating down when we set out, with a strong west wind. We sailed against it.

Neither member of the crew was an accomplished sailor, but there the similarities ended. One man behaved as if he were a guest at a tea party, expecting everything to be done for him. The other kept asking, "What can I do?"

Suddenly a storm came up. After sailing in gale force winds and a driving rainstorm for what seemed like days, two of us safely sailed the boat back—man number two and me.

Both men were successful and respected, but only one had the attributes of a true leader and master of the universe. He was a giver, the other a taker. The taker left our firm before long and has failed to live up to earlier promise. The giver, David Joys, went on to become one of the stars of the firm and is now a very successful headhunter with Heidrick & Struggles.

The superior leader has a vision, sets goals, and gives employees the room to figure out what has to be done and that accountability is necessary to make things happen. Leaders have to work harder, be well prepared for meetings, know more about their client than the client knows, and set an example for everyone else around them. Being a leader is not always easy, and it's not always fun. Leaders are supportive of their people, their predecessors, and their successors. They are positive. While being realistic, great leaders motivate people by seeking the good and the positive in what they are doing. Most of us spend a substantial part of our lives working in an office; it should be fun, stimulating, and rewarding. Good leaders make that happen.

When I started RRA and John Beck was considering investing in it, I asked him what his objective was. "To make you successful," he said. That was a good answer.

If there is uncertainty about who should do what, the leader conveys this simple principle: "Always assume that you are responsible."

Leaders treat others like intelligent, worthy adults with boundless possibilities. Givers are generous and feel gratitude toward those around them who similarly are working on the group's behalf. In sharp contrast, takers want everything for themselves and falsely believe that they are owed everything they receive. Takers manage by instilling fear and self-doubt in others. Takers develop a cult of personality so that it is difficult to disentangle them from the company, the former helping themselves to the riches of the company and the latter sooner or later falling apart.

The attributes of sound leadership are beneficial wherever one is in one's career, because good leadership means taking action and giving credit where credit is due. The unfortunate fact of takers as leaders is that they sometimes reach the top of organizations. And when they do, they can do a lot of damage.

CORPORATE TOYS

Toys—rather than simply poor earnings or poor management—have been the downfall of many CEOs. I have known a number of executives who got so wrapped up in their airplanes that they forgot why they were hired. One of them is deservedly criticized for spending more time at the flight simulator than at the wheel of his own corporation. It is quite conceivable that we will be asked to recruit his replacement. Dependence on "image" is another problem we constantly encounter. Staying competitive, in your personal and your business life, depends more on facts than image. Ultimately, the perception of excellence is meaningless without the reality to back it up, and it can sometimes be harmful, since people expect more out of those with a good image.

Excellence derives from good ideas and the ability of the CEO to recognize them and act on them. Too often, success results in this subconscious reaction: "Don't give me a good idea. It might cost money." Or "Don't give me a good idea. It might force me to exert myself."

OTHER DEADLY SINS

It isn't hard to imagine the personal qualities that get in the way of career advancement. Yes, some people of poor character make it further than they should; just take a look at Wall Street villains like Bernard Madoff or Allen Stanford. But the people around them eventually caught on, and their careers hit a dead end and worse.

Other big character flaws include greed and egocentrism—people who willingly trample on those who get in their way and ultimately do not get the help they need or are sabotaged.

Another critical problem I encounter in leaders is hubris, or overweening pride. Real leaders are, in my experience, very considerate of others. Real leaders don't keep people waiting—in fact, the best ones often show up early. It is a way to show your respect for others. When hubris becomes the defining factor in one's career, that career has commenced its decline. Stay humble and thankful.

At the interpersonal level, other "do nots" include not listening, not saying thank you, not caring about others, using your BlackBerry during a meeting, and not being self-aware. These are all personal qualities that get in the way of obtaining the information you need to make sound decisions and do your job well and to work collaboratively with others.

THE BASICS

We performed a search for a publicly owned utility whose CEO was a very shrewd negotiator. I don't like to admit it, but he persuaded me to undertake several searches for the price of one. Every time we provided him with names and information, his feedback was negative. He slightly changed his requirements and claimed we had not heard him correctly or misunderstood his needs.

His logic, while impressive, was duplicitous. Always polite, his style was nonetheless offensive—there was an edge to everything he said—as was his underlying purpose. I realized that he was carefully establishing a legal reason not to have to pay after we had provided at least two candidates that he hired.

I went on the offensive. We argued over the bill, the requirements, the candidates. The search business, like others, involves compromise, but this was ridiculous. This man's brand of leadership involved intimidation, along with cunning rewording of agreements.

His main strength, if you can call it that, was planting self-doubt in others—the hallmark of the ultimate "taker"—with the objective of avoiding his legal and moral obligations. Eventually he paid at least part of the bill, and then his firm had the nerve to come back to us for a subsequent search. As you may have guessed, we politely declined.

Underscoring these essentials is the importance of determination. In the 1980s, as a devotee of sailing, I participated in a 633-mile race from Newport to Bermuda. I wanted to take my 18-year-old son Jeff, who was a student at the Hotchkiss School, as a crew member. John Lockton, a key member and watch captain of the sailing crew, said he thought Jeff was too young and inexperienced to risk his life on such a long and hazardous race.

Jeff went to see John, and they talked about it. "You will be there in the ocean one night in a driving storm, hanging onto the headstay for dear life," John said. "There will be no moon and no stars. You could easily fall overboard, drown, and disappear into the darkness. I am not sure you're ready for that."

Jeff thanked him and said to me later, "I certainly want to be on your watch, because he's scared to death!" A determined Jeff went with me, and despite some stormy weather, the trip came off without a hitch. He is now helping others as a successful nephrologist in New Haven.

BRIGHT YOUNG PEOPLE

Shortly after I started RRA, I always made a point of hiring bright young people, and a number of them worked for me directly in helping do the business, run the firm, and cover a growing number of offices. Among that group were people like Jeff Bell, now retired in Philadelphia; Ted Kister, still in the search business with David Barrett; Steve Scroggins, an able man with a good financial sense who is still at RRA; and Clarke Murphy, one of the largest producers in the executive search business, and a great sailor, also still at RRA. Murphy, in fact, chartered a 100-foot yacht and entered the transatlantic ocean race to the Isle of Wight this year. He placed third even after the yacht's bowsprit broke, not an easy thing to do.

My last direct helper was an extremely bright and able fellow named Halsey Minor, a University of Virginia graduate like Murphy. Halsey and I worked together during the last two years I was at RRA.

Halsey had the idea that he wanted to start a company based on the advent of technology and the Internet in the early 1990s. Traveling around the globe together in the front of Singapore Airlines jets, we had plenty of time to talk about it. The idea ultimately segued into the formation of a company call CNET, which Halsey started in New York but quickly moved to Northern California. Like all Internet start-ups prior to the bubble burst in the late 1990s, CNET could have been described as a crapshoot. However, if you believe that the right people make the difference, Halsey Minor proved it. Working diligently and without interruption in California, Halsey attracted people; developed the concept; brought in Paul Allen, the cofounder of Microsoft, as a later investor; and built a great company that went public in the mid-1990s.

I was fortunately a small investor in the company at the beginning, and that proved to be a lucky decision. CNET is now part of CBS.

The moral? When you give bright young people a chance, there is no limit to how high they can go.

A friend once told me that "life is the art of drawing without an eraser." In a sense, that is both the reality and the lesson for a corporate recruiter. Leaders are bound by their past decisions and actions; they also provide the basis for calculations about, and evaluations of, candidates.

Ever since I founded RRA, I have believed in the promise of the coming year. And now as head of RSR Partners, I still do. I have come to realize that we all, to some extent, live our lives based on faith: that our cars will start, that airplanes will arrive more or less on time, that politicians will somehow come up with a viable plan for running the country, and that some people will lead and others will follow. The question is how individuals operate within these loose but interdependent relationships, helping others while also helping themselves.

In the same vein, an executive's business performance—the sum of what he or she creates—reflects basic values that are the common denominators of executive search as well as everyday life: the pluses and minuses set down between the day we set out on our own and the time we are no longer active in business.

The basics—life's drawings—are as important now as they have ever been. We are born with certain talents. To develop them to the fullest, in a balanced way, is the key to the equilibrium we seek in whatever we do. Success is measured every day, not at the end of a lifetime.

CONCLUSION

Looking back over 80 years of a very good life, I am very impressed by the number of changes that have taken place in our society in the past several decades. To me, the most important change seems to be that people fear making commitments. Young people are afraid to get married, executives and their boards are worried about their commitments to each other, our young people know little about being committed to serving our country in the right sense, and even Yale University is trying to diminish its commitment to athletics, and particularly football, having virtually originated the game in the United States.

Those people who were young and got older and succeeded in establishing the right equilibrium in their own lives were the people who were able to recognize the importance of commitments to others, be it family, business associates, or causes they support. People who are respected are people who are viewed as being leaders, and leaders make commitments. They put themselves on the line. They don't hedge every bet.

If you want to succeed in life and in business, you should commit yourself to those people and organizations and institutions that appeal to you and that you respect. You will not always be pleased; you will often be disappointed. But if you made the right decision to begin with, you will be more than vindicated over a period of time.

At this writing, unemployment in the United States is 8.3 percent, which of course does not count the millions of people who have given up looking for jobs. It makes me wonder what has happened to the loyalty of the employers who hire people in the first place and then let them go. It makes me wonder why older people don't still have the unbridled faith in bright young people that we had in previous years. And I often wonder why the unemployed aren't able to create an opportunity for themselves, as the pioneers in this country did four centuries ago.

Why have the values that made this country so great fallen apart? Opportunity is everywhere if you look for it. America needs to return to its core values and get back to work. We need to hold ourselves responsible for the situation and not others. We should help others strengthen themselves. We need to get back to basics and stop looking over our shoulder but look in the mirror. We need to tell ourselves that, yes, I can make this happen and I will. It doesn't matter what your social, educational, or financial background is. What does matter is believing in yourself and recapturing the spirit of self-determination.

Commitments bring people a feeling of security. You know whom you can rely on when things get rough. You know who your friends are, and they know you. Not long ago, I attended a lecture at Yale given by an eminent psychiatrist who was talking about what constitutes happiness among people. She made the point that unless you know who your eight great-grandparents were, you really don't know where you came from. And if you don't know where you came from, you don't have a feeling of stability or belonging. It doesn't matter what your circumstances are; it is the fact that knowing how things happened is what gives people a feeling of security and equilibrium. I think this concept pertains to relationships in the business world as much as it does in any other part of life. I am committed to those I work with, and they are committed to our firm.

We are at a moment in time when we can still take back the great values that made this country and corporate America the envy of the entire world. Each of us can do it.

Upon reviewing my own career, I feel that I have been extremely fortunate. Being raised in a simple way with modest means, but also with great educational opportunities laced with summer jobs since I was 13, gave me a sense of the best things the world has to offer. Knowing that I was neither a great analyst nor mathematician and only a mediocre athlete, I found my niche by gradually accommodating my lifestyle to the areas that intrigued me and in which I felt the most comfortable. Anyone can do this. When I retired from my first firm, RRA, I probably was in a position to coast for the rest of my life.

But I was attracted by the magnetism and appeal of the executive search business and the fascinating panoply of people you meet both as clients and as candidates. As I built my first firm and am currently building the second, I am equally attracted by the terrific, uplifting people with whom one can become associated. Likes and dislikes are always a matter of individual style, and I am fortunate that I feel that I have found my niche. What I am doing is better than playing golf every day or sitting on an ocean liner contemplating the endless scope of the horizon.

The real satisfaction in life comes from trying to do a simple thing well and keeping at it. After noticing that many of the great leaders in my hometown of Greenwich were running companies, were deeply involved in civic activities, or were in politics well into their later years, I was inspired to attempt to do the same. The prospects of the United States have never been brighter in spite of obvious current concerns. Europe, Asia, and South America are also learning from their mistakes. Recent innovations in social media have empowered a new generation to develop relationships and connections with each other in an unprecedented way. As a result, technology is forcing us to develop more transactional, shallower, and less intimate relationships. Some have argued that the war for talent will be played on a technological battlefield and that the need for executive recruiting will diminish. I would contend that the need for people to assess and discover the soul and depth of an individual will never be greater as the world continues to connect in an impersonal way.

A great executive recruiter is like a submarine commander who has the ability to raise his periscope and get a 360-degree look at the world. Once he sees the whole picture, he takes aim and fires. That is the essence of the search business. This analogy applies to all major business decisions, including picking the best people. It won't go away. That is why I am so excited about the future of this business.

INDEX

ABOUT THE AUTHOR

Russell S. Reynolds, Jr., is the CEO of RSR Partners, a senior-level retained executive and board search firm based in Greenwich, CT, with offices in New York, Cleveland, Chicago, and Los Angeles. Russ Reynolds is the founder of Russell Reynolds Associates, from which he retired in the 1990s. He is considered one of the leaders of today's executive search business and has counseled chairmen, presidents, and CEOs of hundreds of companies throughout the world. He has recently been featured on CNBC's *Closing Bell* and has appeared on the *Today* show, the *CBS Evening News*, and the BBC. A graduate of Yale, Mr. Reynolds was a navigator bombardier in the Strategic Air Command and later a commercial banker at J.P. Morgan before entering the search business. He and his wife live in Greenwich, CT, and have 3 married children and 11 grandchildren. He published his first book, *Loyal to the Land*, in 1990. Mr. Reynolds is a former cruising/racing sailor and enjoys skiing, racquet sports, and great music.

5/3/12   4:50 PM